Relocating to France: A Comprehensive Guide f

Hubert McDonald

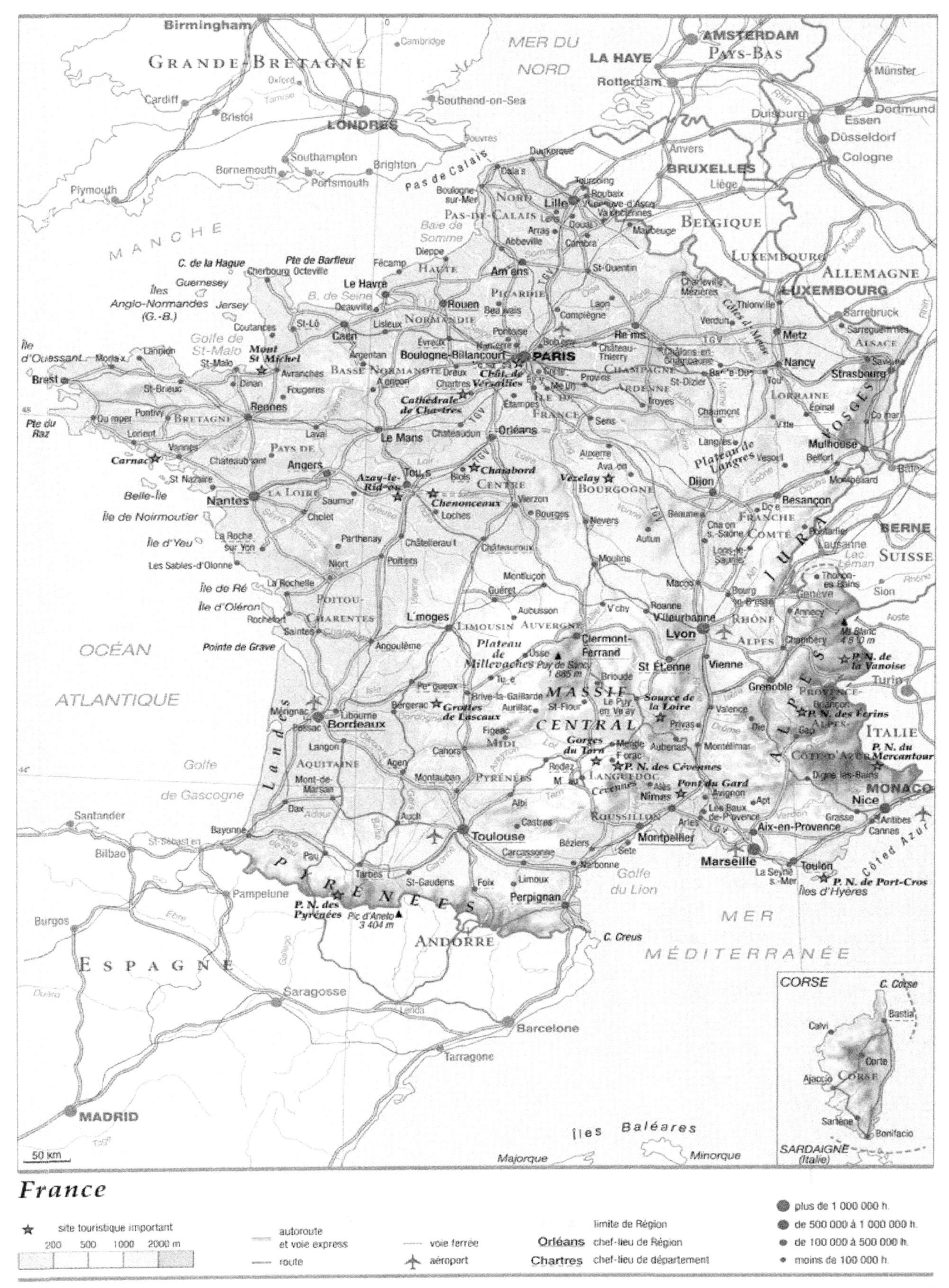

GRANDE-BRETAGNE
MER DU NORD
AMSTERDAM
PAYS-BAS
LA HAYE
Rotterdam
Birmingham
Cambridge
Oxford
Cardiff
Bristol
LONDRES
Southend-on-Sea
Southampton
Brighton
Bornemouth
Portsmouth
Plymouth
Pas de Calais
Dunkerque
Calais
Boulogne-sur-Mer
NORD
PAS-DE-CALAIS
Lille
Tourcoing
Roubaix
Valenciennes
Arras
Douai
Cambrai
Maubeuge
Anvers
BRUXELLES
Liège
BELGIQUE
Münster
Dortmund
Essen
Duisburg
Düsseldorf
Cologne
MANCHE
Baie de Somme
Abbeville
Dieppe
Amiens
St-Quentin
Charleville-Mézières
LUXEMBOURG
ALLEMAGNE
C. de la Hague
Pte de Barfleur
Fécamp
Cherbourg Octeville
Le Havre
B. de Seine
Deauville
Rouen
PICARDIE
Beauvais
Laon
Compiègne
Thionville
Sarrebruck
Îles Anglo-Normandes (G.-B.)
Guernesey
Jersey
Coutances
St-Lô
Lisieux
NORMANDIE
Caen
Évreux
Pontoise
Reims
Verdun
Metz
ALSACE
Golfe de St-Malo
Île d'Ouessant
Morlaix
Lannion
St-Malo
Mont St Michel
Brest
Argentan
Boulogne-Billancourt
PARIS
Château-Thierry
Châlons-en-Champagne
Nancy
Saverne
Strasbourg
BASSE-NORMANDIE
Dreux
Chât. de Versailles
Évry
Melun
Provins
CHAMPAGNE-ARDENNE
St-Dizier
Bar-le-Duc
Toul
St-Brieuc
Dinan
Avranches
Fougères
Alençon
Chartres
Cathédrale de Chartres
ÎLE-DE-FRANCE
Troyes
LORRAINE
VOSGES
Pte du Raz
Quimper
Pontivy
BRETAGNE
Rennes
Étampes
Sens
Chaumont
Épinal
Colmar
Lorient
Laval
Le Mans
Châteaudun
Orléans
Vitré
Mulhouse
Carnac
Vannes
PAYS DE LA LOIRE
Châteaubriant
Angers
Tours
Chambord
Blois
Auxerre
Avallon
Langres
Plateau de Langres
Vesoul
Belfort
Bâle
St Nazaire
Azay-le-Rideau
CENTRE
Vézelay
BOURGOGNE
Dijon
Montbéliard
Belle-Île
Nantes
Saumur
Chenonceaux
Vierzon
Besançon
Île de Noirmoutier
Cholet
Loches
Bourges
Nevers
Beaune
Dole
FRANCHE-COMTÉ
BERNE
Île d'Yeu
La Roche-sur-Yon
Parthenay
Châtellerault
Autun
Chalon-s.-Saône
Pontarlier
SUISSE
Les Sables-d'Olonne
Niort
Poitiers
Châteauroux
Moulins
Lons-le-Saunier
JURA
Lausanne
Lac Léman
Île de Ré
La Rochelle
POITOU-CHARENTES
Montluçon
Guéret
Mâcon
Bourg-en-Bresse
Thonon-les-Bains
Genève
Sion
Île d'Oléron
Rochefort
Saintes
Limoges
LIMOUSIN
AUVERGNE
Aubusson
Vichy
Roanne
Villeurbanne
RHÔNE
Annecy
Aoste
OCÉAN ATLANTIQUE
Pointe de Grave
Angoulême
Plateau de Millevaches
Ussel
Puy de Sancy 1 885 m
Clermont-Ferrand
Lyon
ALPES
Chambéry
Mt Blanc 4 810 m
St Étienne
Vienne
P. N. de la Vanoise
Brioude
Tulle
Périgueux
Brive-la-Gaillarde
MASSIF CENTRAL
Source de la Loire
Grenoble
PROVENCE-ALPES-CÔTE-D'AZUR
Turin
Mérignac
Pessac
Libourne
Bordeaux
Bergerac
Grottes de Lascaux
Aurillac
St-Flour
Le Puy en Velay
Valence
Briançon
P. N. des Écrins
Figeac
Privas
Die
Gap
ITALIE
Langon
MIDI
Cahors
Gorges du Tarn
Mende
Florac
Aubenas
Montélimar
P. N. du Mercantour
Golfe de Gascogne
AQUITAINE
Landes
Agen
Rodez
P. N. des Cévennes
CÔTE-D'AZUR
Digne-les-Bains
Mont-de-Marsan
Montauban
PYRÉNÉES
Millau
LANGUEDOC
Cévennes
Alès
Pont du Gard
Avignon
Nîmes
MONACO
Nice
Santander
Dax
Albi
Castres
Apt
Les Baux-de-Provence
Grasse
Antibes
Cannes
Bayonne
Auch
Toulouse
ROUSSILLON
Arles
Aix-en-Provence
Bilbao
St-Sébastien
Pau
Carcassonne
Béziers
Montpellier
Marseille
Côte d'Azur
Tarbes
St-Gaudens
Foix
Narbonne
Sète
Golfe du Lion
La Seyne-s.-Mer
Toulon
P. N. de Port-Cros
Îles d'Hyères
Pampelune
P. N. des Pyrénées
Limoux
Perpignan
Pic d'Aneto 3 404 m
Burgos
ANDORRE
C. Creus
MER MÉDITERRANÉE
ESPAGNE
Saragosse
CORSE
C. Corse
Bastia
Calvi
Corte
Ajaccio
Sartène
Bonifacio
SARDAIGNE (Italie)
Lérida
Barcelone
Tarragone
MADRID
Îles Baléares
Majorque
Minorque
50 km

France

site touristique important
200 500 1000 2000 m
autoroute et voie express
route
voie ferrée
aéroport
limite de Région
Orléans chef-lieu de Région
Chartres chef-lieu de département
plus de 1 000 000 h.
de 500 000 à 1 000 000 h.
de 100 000 à 500 000 h.
moins de 100 000 h.

Table of Contents:

Preface

Relocating to a new country is an adventure laden with excitement, challenges, and the promise of new beginnings. Yet, when that country is as rich in history, culture, and allure as France, the journey takes on an entirely unique dimension. Welcome to "Relocating to France," a comprehensive guide crafted to be your trusted companion on this transformative odyssey.

France has long captivated the imagination of the world with its exquisite cuisine, picturesque landscapes, and artistic heritage. From the bustling streets of Paris to the quaint villages of Provence, every corner of this nation holds treasures waiting to be discovered. However, beneath its romantic façade lies a complex tapestry of customs, bureaucracy, and social norms that can be daunting to navigate, especially for those contemplating a move from afar.

This book is designed to be more than just a practical manual; it's a roadmap infused with insights, anecdotes, and firsthand experiences to illuminate the path toward a successful relocation. Whether you're dreaming of sipping espresso at a sidewalk café in Montmartre or strolling along the sun-drenched shores of the French Riviera, the journey begins here.

Within these pages, you'll find invaluable advice on everything from visa requirements and housing options to cultural etiquette and language tips. From the intricacies of French bureaucracy to the nuances of daily life, each chapter is crafted to empower you with the knowledge and confidence needed to embrace your new life in France fully.

Drawing upon the collective wisdom of expatriates, seasoned travelers, and local experts, this book aims to provide a holistic understanding of what it means to relocate to France. Whether you're a student embarking on a semester abroad, a professional pursuing career opportunities, or a retiree seeking a tranquil retreat, the insights shared here are tailored to meet your unique needs and aspirations.

As you embark on this exhilarating journey, remember that every challenge is an opportunity for growth, and every setback is a chance to learn. Embrace the unfamiliar, cherish the moments of discovery, and allow yourself to be enchanted by the timeless allure of La Belle France.

Bon voyage, and may your relocation to France be a chapter in your life story filled with joy, fulfillment, and unforgettable experiences.

Bienvenue en France!

Introduction

Understanding the Decision to Relocate

Relocating to a new country is a significant life decision that involves various factors and considerations. France, with its rich history, diverse culture, and promising opportunities, often emerges as an attractive destination for individuals and families seeking a fresh start. Understanding the motivations behind the decision to relocate to France can shed light on the intricate dynamics involved in such a transformative step.

1. Cultural allure: France is renowned worldwide for its cultural richness, including its art, cuisine, fashion, and architecture. The prospect of immersing oneself in this vibrant cultural tapestry can be a compelling reason to relocate. From strolling through picturesque streets lined with charming cafes to exploring world-class museums and galleries, France offers an unparalleled cultural experience that resonates with many.

2. Quality of life: The French lifestyle, with its emphasis on leisure, gastronomy, and work-life balance, appeals to those seeking a higher quality of life. The country's healthcare system, social services, and robust infrastructure contribute to a sense of security and well-being. Moreover, the scenic landscapes, from the Mediterranean coast to the picturesque countryside, offer opportunities for relaxation and outdoor activities.

3. Professional opportunities: France is home to numerous multinational companies, thriving industries, and burgeoning startups, making it an attractive destination for career advancement. Cities like Paris, Lyon, and Toulouse serve as hubs for various sectors, including technology, finance, fashion, and hospitality. The prospect of pursuing career opportunities in these dynamic environments motivates many individuals to relocate.

4. Educational pursuits: France boasts a prestigious education system, with renowned universities and institutions offering a wide range of academic programs. For students and academics alike, the opportunity to study or conduct research in fields such as art, science, literature, and engineering serves as a driving force behind the decision to relocate.

5. Family considerations: Family ties often play a crucial role in the decision to relocate. Whether it's joining a spouse or partner already established in France, providing children with access to quality education and cultural experiences, or reuniting with extended family members, familial bonds can strongly influence the relocation process.

6. Political and social stability: France's reputation as a democratic nation with a commitment to liberty, equality, and fraternity attracts individuals seeking political stability and social cohesion. The country's long history of activism and cultural diversity fosters an environment conducive to personal growth, social integration, and civic engagement.

7. EU citizenship and mobility: For citizens of European Union (EU) member states, relocating to France offers the advantage of EU citizenship, facilitating freedom of movement within the Schengen Area and access to various rights and privileges. This mobility can be particularly appealing in a globalized world where cross-border opportunities abound.

8. Adventure and exploration: Ultimately, the decision to relocate to France may stem from a sense of adventure and the desire to explore new horizons. Whether it's mastering the French language, adapting to a different way of life, or embarking on a journey of self-discovery, the prospect of embracing the unknown can be a powerful motivator.

In conclusion, the decision to relocate to France is a multifaceted process shaped by individual aspirations, professional ambitions, cultural affinities, and personal circumstances. By understanding the diverse motivations behind this choice, we gain insight into the complex interplay of factors that drive individuals and families to embark on a new chapter in one of the world's most captivating destinations.

Overview of France as a Destination

France, with its rich history, cultural heritage, stunning landscapes, and world-renowned cuisine, stands as one of the most sought-after destinations for travelers from across the globe. Situated in Western Europe, France offers a diverse array of experiences, ranging from vibrant cities to picturesque countryside retreats and charming coastal towns. Here's an overview of what makes France an irresistible destination:

Cultural Heritage:

France boasts a cultural tapestry woven with centuries of history, evident in its magnificent landmarks, museums, and artistic achievements. Visitors can marvel at iconic landmarks such as the Eiffel Tower, Notre-Dame Cathedral, and the Palace of Versailles. The country is also home to an exceptional array of museums, including the Louvre, Musée d'Orsay, and Centre Pompidou, housing some of the world's most significant art collections.

Gastronomy:

French cuisine is celebrated globally for its exquisite flavors, culinary techniques, and emphasis on fresh, high-quality ingredients. From gourmet dining experiences in Michelin-starred restaurants to sampling street food at bustling markets, France offers a gastronomic journey like no other. Indulge in delectable pastries, savory cheeses, fine wines, and regional specialties that vary from the coasts to the mountains.

Scenic Landscapes:

France's diverse geography encompasses everything from rolling vineyards and lush countryside to majestic mountain ranges and pristine coastlines. Travelers can explore the picturesque villages of Provence, wander through the lavender fields of the French Alps, or relax on the sun-kissed beaches of the French Riviera. Outdoor enthusiasts can also indulge in a myriad of activities, including hiking, skiing, cycling, and sailing.

Charming Villages and Towns:

Beyond its bustling cities, France is dotted with enchanting villages and towns that exude old-world charm and tranquility. Explore the medieval streets of Carcassonne, wander through the fairytale-like village of Eguisheim in Alsace, or meander along the cobblestone lanes of Mont-Saint-Michel. Each region offers a unique ambiance, architecture, and culinary delights waiting to be discovered.

Art and Fashion:
France has long been synonymous with art, fashion, and style. Paris, the capital city, is a global hub for fashion, design, and haute couture, with prestigious fashion houses, boutiques, and flagship stores lining its boulevards. Art aficionados can immerse themselves in the thriving contemporary art scene, attend world-class fashion shows, or explore the ateliers of renowned designers.

Cultural Festivals and Events:
Throughout the year, France hosts an array of cultural festivals, events, and celebrations that showcase its diverse heritage and traditions. From the Cannes Film Festival and the Tour de France to vibrant carnivals and music festivals, there's always something happening in France to captivate visitors of all interests.

Transportation and Accessibility:
France boasts a well-developed transportation network, making it easy for travelers to explore the country. High-speed trains connect major cities, while an extensive network of highways and scenic routes makes road trips a popular option. Additionally, France is served by numerous international airports, with Paris being a major gateway for travelers arriving from around the world.

In conclusion, France offers a perfect blend of history, culture, cuisine, and natural beauty, making it a quintessential destination for travelers seeking unforgettable experiences. Whether you're exploring its iconic landmarks, savoring its culinary delights, or simply soaking in its scenic landscapes, France promises to enchant and inspire visitors at every turn.

Chapter 1

Preparing for the Move

1.1 Assessing Your Reasons for Relocation

Relocating to another country, like France, is a significant life decision that requires careful consideration and planning. Whether you're drawn to the cultural richness, professional opportunities, or simply seeking a change of pace, it's crucial to assess your reasons for making such a move. Here are some key factors to consider when evaluating your decision to relocate to France:

1. Cultural Adjustment: France boasts a diverse cultural landscape, from its renowned cuisine and art to its distinct regional traditions. Ask yourself how comfortable you are with adapting to a new culture and whether you're prepared for the potential challenges of language barriers and cultural differences.

2. Career and Employment Opportunities: Evaluate the professional landscape in France and assess whether your skills and qualifications align with the job market. Research industries that are thriving in the country and explore potential employment options or entrepreneurial opportunities.

3. Quality of Life: Consider how your lifestyle may change in France compared to your current location. Take into account factors such as healthcare, education, cost of living, and work-life balance. Assess whether the lifestyle offerings in France align with your personal preferences and priorities.

4. Legal and Administrative Requirements: Familiarize yourself with the legal and administrative procedures involved in relocating to France, including visa requirements, residency permits, taxation, and healthcare enrollment. Ensure you have a clear understanding of the paperwork and processes necessary for a smooth transition.

5. Social Support Network: Reflect on your existing social support network and consider how relocating to France may impact your relationships with friends and family. Explore opportunities to build new connections and seek out expatriate communities or networking groups to help ease the transition.

6. Personal Fulfillment: Assess whether relocating to France aligns with your long-term personal goals and aspirations. Consider how the move may contribute to your personal growth, fulfillment, and overall well-being.

7. Financial Considerations: Evaluate the financial implications of relocating to France, including housing costs, taxation, currency exchange rates, and potential changes to your income or financial stability. Create a realistic budget and financial plan to ensure you're prepared for the financial aspects of the move.

8. Risk Assessment: Consider the potential risks and uncertainties associated with relocating to France, such as political instability, economic fluctuations, or unexpected challenges. Develop contingency plans and strategies to mitigate these risks and ensure a smooth transition.

By carefully assessing your reasons for relocating to France and considering these key factors, you can make an informed decision that aligns with your goals, values, and aspirations. Remember to seek advice from professionals, expatriates, and individuals with experience in international relocation to help guide you through the process. With thorough planning and preparation, your move to France can be a rewarding and enriching experience.

1.2 Researching French Culture and Lifestyle

Introduction:

France, with its rich history, diverse landscapes, and vibrant culture, has long been a beacon of inspiration for travelers and researchers alike. From the cobblestone streets of Paris to the sun-kissed vineyards of Bordeaux, every corner of France offers a unique glimpse into its captivating culture and lifestyle. Embarking on a journey to explore French culture and lifestyle is not only an adventure but also an opportunity to delve deep into the essence of this enchanting country.

Understanding French Culture:

At the heart of French culture lies a profound appreciation for art, literature, and philosophy. From the iconic works of Claude Monet to the literary masterpieces of Victor Hugo, France has been a cradle of creativity for centuries. Researching French culture involves immersing oneself in its art galleries, museums, and libraries, where the echoes of history resonate with each stroke of the brush and turn of the page.

Language is another integral aspect of French culture. As the language of love and diplomacy, French holds a special place in the hearts of its people. Learning the nuances of the French language opens doors to deeper connections with locals and a better understanding of their way of life.

Exploring French Lifestyle:

The French way of life, often romanticized and admired, is a harmonious blend of tradition and modernity. From leisurely strolls along the Seine River to indulgent culinary experiences in quaint bistros, the French lifestyle celebrates the simple joys of everyday living.

Cuisine is an integral part of French lifestyle, where meals are not just sustenance but experiences to be savored and shared. Researching French cuisine involves exploring local markets, sampling regional delicacies, and learning the art of pairing food with the finest wines.

The concept of "joie de vivre" or the joy of living permeates every aspect of French lifestyle. Whether it's enjoying a picnic in the countryside or sipping espresso at a sidewalk café, the French embrace life with a sense of spontaneity and appreciation for the moment.

Practical Research Tips:

To make the most of your research on French culture and lifestyle, consider the following tips:

1. Immerse yourself in the local community by participating in cultural events, festivals, and workshops.
2. Seek out authentic experiences off the beaten path, away from tourist traps, to gain a deeper understanding of French life.
3. Engage with locals through language exchange programs or guided tours led by knowledgeable residents.
4. Document your experiences through photography, journaling, or blogging to preserve memories and insights gained during your research.

Researching French culture and lifestyle is a rewarding endeavor that offers a profound appreciation for the richness and diversity of this captivating country. Whether you're exploring the historic streets of Paris or savoring the flavors of Provence, each experience brings you closer to the essence of French life. So pack your bags, embrace the adventure, and embark on a journey to discover the magic of France firsthand. Bon voyage!

1.3 Financial Planning and Budgeting

I hope this message finds you well. As your business expands its operations into France, it's essential to establish robust financial planning and budgeting strategies to ensure sustainable growth and success in this new market. Effective financial management is crucial for navigating the unique challenges and opportunities presented by operating in France's dynamic business landscape.

Here are some key considerations and recommendations for financial planning and budgeting tailored to your venture in France:

1. Market Analysis and Localization: Conduct a thorough market analysis to understand the nuances of the French market, including consumer preferences, regulatory frameworks, taxation policies, and competitive landscape. Localization of your financial plans and budgets is critical to align with the specific requirements and expectations of French stakeholders.

2. Budget Allocation: Allocate your financial resources strategically, considering both short-term operational needs and long-term growth objectives. Prioritize investments in areas such as marketing and localization efforts to enhance brand awareness and adapt your products or services to the French market.

3. Taxation and Compliance: Familiarize yourself with France's taxation system and ensure compliance with local tax laws and regulations. Seek professional advice to optimize your tax structure and identify available incentives or exemptions that can lower your tax burden.

4. Currency Risk Management: Given the potential impact of currency fluctuations on your financial performance, consider implementing hedging strategies to mitigate currency risk exposure. Monitor exchange rate movements closely and adjust your financial plans accordingly to minimize adverse effects on profitability.

5. Financial Forecasting and Monitoring: Develop comprehensive financial forecasts to anticipate revenue streams, expenses, and cash flow dynamics in the French market. Regularly monitor your financial performance against budgeted targets and adjust your plans as needed to stay on track towards your goals.

6. Risk Management: Identify and assess potential risks to your business in France, such as regulatory changes, economic instability, or geopolitical uncertainties. Implement risk management strategies to mitigate these risks and safeguard your financial health.

7. Investment in Talent and Infrastructure: Invest in recruiting and retaining local talent with the expertise and cultural understanding necessary to drive your business's success in France. Additionally, allocate resources to develop robust infrastructure and operational capabilities to support your expansion efforts effectively.

8. Financial Contingency Planning: Anticipate unforeseen challenges or disruptions that may impact your business operations in France. Establish contingency plans and allocate financial reserves to address emergencies or unexpected events proactively.

By implementing these financial planning and budgeting strategies, you can enhance your business's resilience and competitiveness in the French market while maximizing opportunities for growth and profitability.

Should you require further assistance or guidance on financial matters related to your expansion into France, please don't hesitate to reach out. Our team is here to support you every step of the way.

1.4 Understanding Visa and Residency Requirements

France, renowned for its rich culture, stunning landscapes, and culinary delights, attracts millions of visitors and expatriates each year. Whether you're planning a short-term visit or considering making France your new home, understanding the visa and residency requirements is crucial. Navigating the intricate process can seem daunting, but with proper information, it becomes manageable.

Short-Term Visits:

For short-term stays, typically less than 90 days within a 180-day period, citizens of many countries, including those within the European Union (EU), the European Economic Area (EEA), and Switzerland, do not require visas. However, citizens from other countries may need a Schengen visa. This visa allows entry to the Schengen Area, which encompasses most EU countries, including France.

Long-Term Stays:

If you plan to stay in France for longer than 90 days, you'll need to apply for a long-stay visa or a residence permit. The type of visa or permit you need depends on various factors, such as your nationality, the purpose of your stay, and whether you plan to work or study.

1. Long-Stay Visa (Visa de Long Séjour):

- This visa is suitable for those intending to stay in France for more than 90 days.
- Different categories of long-stay visas exist, including visas for family reunification, work, study, and entrepreneurship.
- The application process typically involves submitting various documents, including proof of accommodation, financial means, and health insurance.

2. Residence Permit (Titre de Séjour):

- After arriving in France with a long-stay visa, you must apply for a residence permit within a specific timeframe.
- The process varies depending on the type of permit you're applying for, such as a student residence permit, work permit, or family reunification permit.
- Renewal of the residence permit is usually necessary annually or every few years, depending on the permit's validity period.

Work and Residence:

If your purpose for residing in France is work-related, additional requirements come into play. Employers may need to sponsor your visa or residence permit, and you might have to demonstrate your qualifications and expertise to obtain a work permit. France prioritizes EU/EEA citizens and their family members for employment opportunities, but non-EU/EEA nationals can still find work under specific conditions.

Healthcare and Social Security:

France boasts one of the world's most renowned healthcare systems, and residents enjoy access to quality medical care. Those staying in France for an extended period may need to contribute to the social security system, providing access to healthcare, unemployment benefits, and other social services.

Understanding visa and residency requirements in France is essential for a smooth transition, whether you're planning a short-term visit or aiming for long-term residency. Thorough research and proper documentation are key to successfully navigating the process. With its charm, opportunities, and quality of life, France continues to attract individuals from around the globe, making it a popular destination for both tourism and relocation.

1.5 Learning the French Language and Cultural Etiquette

Learning the French language and understanding cultural etiquette are essential for anyone planning to visit or live in France. The French language is not only a means of communication but also a gateway to understanding French culture, history, and society. Moreover, being familiar with French etiquette and social norms can help you navigate social interactions and build meaningful relationships with locals. In this guide, we'll explore tips for learning the French language and understanding cultural etiquette in France.

1. Learning the French Language:

a. Language Schools: Consider enrolling in a language school or taking private lessons to learn French. Immersive programs where you're surrounded by the language can be particularly effective.

b. Online Resources: Utilize online resources such as language learning apps, websites, and podcasts to supplement your learning. Apps like Duolingo, Babbel, and Rosetta Stone offer interactive lessons.

c. Practice Regularly: Practice speaking, listening, reading, and writing in French regularly. Try to immerse yourself in the language by watching French movies, listening to French music, and reading French literature.

d. Language Exchange: Participate in language exchange programs where you can practice speaking with native French speakers in exchange for helping them learn your native language.

e. Cultural Understanding: Learn about French culture, history, and customs as they are closely intertwined with the language. Understanding cultural nuances will enhance your language learning experience.

2. Understanding Cultural Etiquette:

a. Greetings: In France, greetings are important. When meeting someone, it's customary to shake hands, with a slight nod of the head. Use "Bonjour" (good morning/afternoon) and "Bonsoir" (good evening) depending on the time of day.

b. Formality: Address people using appropriate titles such as "Monsieur" (Mr.), "Madame" (Mrs.), or "Mademoiselle" (Miss), followed by their last name until invited to use their first name.

c. Dining Etiquette: French dining etiquette is formal. Wait to be seated and keep your hands on the table, not in your lap. Avoid starting to eat until the host begins or indicates you should. Use utensils properly and keep your hands visible.

d. Personal Space: French people value their personal space. Avoid standing too close or initiating physical contact unless invited to do so.

e. Punctuality: Punctuality is appreciated in France. Arrive on time for appointments, meetings, and social gatherings.

f. Language Use: Attempt to speak French, even if it's just basic phrases. French people appreciate the effort, even if you make mistakes.

g. Politeness: Politeness is highly regarded in French culture. Use "please" ("s'il vous plaît") and "thank you" ("merci") frequently.

h. Dress Code: Dress neatly and appropriately for different occasions. French fashion tends to be stylish yet understated.

Learning the French language and understanding cultural etiquette are invaluable skills for anyone wishing to immerse themselves in French culture or visit France. By investing time and effort into language learning and familiarizing yourself with cultural norms, you'll not only enhance your travel experience but also build meaningful connections with the people you encounter in France. Embrace the opportunity to learn and adapt, and you'll find yourself appreciating the richness of French language and culture even more.

Chapter 2

Legal and Administrative Processes

2.1 Obtaining the Appropriate Visa

France, with its rich history, vibrant culture, and thriving economy, attracts millions of visitors each year. Whether you're planning to study, work, or simply explore this beautiful country, understanding the visa requirements and navigating the application process is crucial. Obtaining the appropriate visa ensures a smooth entry and stay in France, allowing you to make the most of your experience. In this guide, we'll walk you through the essential steps to secure the right visa for your purpose.

1. Determine Your Visa Type:

- France offers various types of visas tailored to different purposes, including tourism, study, work, family reunion, and more.
- Identify the specific visa category that aligns with your intentions and duration of stay in France.

2. Research Visa Requirements:

- Visit the official website of the French consulate or embassy in your country to access detailed information about visa requirements.
- Understand the documentation needed, such as passport validity, proof of accommodation, financial means, travel itinerary, and health insurance coverage.

3. Compile Necessary Documents:

- Gather all required documents meticulously, ensuring they meet the specified criteria and are presented in the correct format.
- Pay close attention to any additional requirements specific to your visa category, such as enrollment in a French institution for student visas or a job offer for work visas.

4. Initiate the Application Process:

- Schedule an appointment at the nearest French consulate or embassy to submit your visa application.
- Complete the application form accurately, providing truthful information and double-checking for any errors or omissions.
- Be prepared to pay the visa application fee, which varies depending on the type and duration of the visa.

5. Attend Visa Interview (if required):

- Some visa categories may necessitate an in-person interview as part of the application process.
- Approach the interview with confidence, being prepared to discuss your intentions for visiting France and providing any requested information or clarification.

6. Await Visa Processing:

- After submitting your application and attending any required interviews, patiently await a decision on your visa.
- Visa processing times can vary depending on various factors, including the volume of applications and the complexity of your case.

7. Receive Your Visa:

- Once your visa application is approved, collect your passport with the affixed visa from the consulate or embassy.
- Carefully review the visa to ensure accuracy in the dates and conditions of stay before traveling to France.

8. Comply with Visa Conditions:

- Upon arrival in France, adhere to the conditions stipulated on your visa, including the duration of stay and any restrictions on employment or study.
- Keep your passport and visa documentation secure throughout your stay in France, as you may be required to present them during routine checks by authorities.

Navigating the visa process in France can seem daunting, but with thorough research, careful preparation, and adherence to requirements, obtaining the appropriate visa becomes a manageable task. By following the steps outlined in this guide and seeking assistance from the relevant authorities when needed, you can embark on your journey to France with confidence, ready to immerse yourself in its rich culture and unforgettable experiences.

2.2 Understanding Residence Permits and Registration

France, renowned for its rich cultural heritage, exquisite cuisine, and picturesque landscapes, is a popular destination for individuals seeking to reside within its borders. However, to establish legal residency in France, understanding the intricacies of residence permits and registration processes is essential. Whether you are relocating for work, study, or personal reasons, navigating the bureaucracy of French immigration laws can be daunting. Here's a comprehensive guide to help you understand residence permits and registration requirements in France.

Residence Permit Categories:

1. Short-stay Visa (Visa de court séjour): Designed for individuals intending to stay in France for less than 90 days, this visa is suitable for tourists, business travelers, and short-term visitors. It does not grant residency rights beyond the specified duration.

2. Long-stay Visa (Visa de long séjour): For stays exceeding 90 days, this visa is required. It's divided into several categories based on the purpose of stay, such as work, study, family reunion, or exceptional circumstances.

3. Residence Permit (Titre de séjour): Upon arrival in France with a long-stay visa, individuals must apply for a residence permit within a designated time frame, typically within the first few months of arrival. The type of residence permit depends on the purpose of stay and may include permits for work, studies, family reunification, or asylum.

Registration Process:

1. Arrival in France: Upon arrival, individuals with long-stay visas must undergo various administrative procedures to formalize their stay in France.

2. Proof of Address: One of the primary requirements for obtaining a residence permit is proof of accommodation in France. This can be in the form of a lease agreement, utility bills, or a letter of accommodation from a host.

3. Document Submission: Applicants must gather necessary documents, including passport copies, visa documents, proof of financial means, and any other documents specific to their visa category. These documents are typically submitted to the local Prefecture or designated immigration office.

4. Biometric Data Collection: As part of the application process, applicants may be required to provide biometric data such as fingerprints and photographs.

5. Interview (if applicable): Depending on the visa category and individual circumstances, applicants may need to attend an interview to provide further information or clarify aspects of their application.

6. Processing Time: The processing time for residence permit applications varies depending on the workload of the immigration authorities and the complexity of the case. It's advisable to submit applications well in advance to avoid any delays.

7. Notification of Decision: Once the application is processed, applicants will receive notification of the decision either by mail or email. If approved, they will be issued a residence permit allowing them to legally reside in France.

Renewal and Extension:

Residence permits in France are typically issued for a limited duration, and renewal or extension may be necessary to continue legal residency. It's essential to be aware of the expiry date of the residence permit and initiate renewal procedures well in advance.

Conclusion:

Understanding the intricacies of residence permits and registration processes is crucial for anyone intending to establish legal residency in France. By familiarizing yourself with the various visa categories, documentation requirements, and administrative procedures, you can navigate the immigration process more effectively. Seeking guidance from immigration professionals or legal experts can also provide valuable assistance in ensuring a smooth transition to life in France.

2.3 Navigating French Bureaucracy

Navigating French bureaucracy can seem like a daunting task for expatriates and visitors alike. However, with patience, preparation, and understanding, it can be managed effectively. Here are some tips to help you navigate the intricacies of French bureaucracy:

1. **Research and Understand the System:** Before diving into any bureaucratic process, take the time to research and understand the specific requirements and procedures involved. Each department or agency may have its own set of rules and paperwork, so knowing what to expect can save you time and frustration.

2. **Gather Necessary Documents:** French bureaucracy often requires a plethora of paperwork. Make sure you have all the necessary documents, such as identification, proof of address, and relevant forms, before you begin any administrative process. Missing paperwork can significantly delay your progress.

3. **Learn the Language:** While it's not always a requirement, having a basic understanding of French can be immensely helpful when dealing with bureaucracy. Many forms and documents may only be available in French, and some officials may not speak English fluently. Consider taking language classes or hiring a translator if needed.

4. **Be Patient and Persistent:** French bureaucracy is notorious for its slow pace and long waiting times. Prepare yourself for delays and be patient throughout the

process. It may take multiple visits or phone calls to resolve an issue, so persistence is key.

5. Seek Assistance if Needed: If you're feeling overwhelmed or confused, don't hesitate to seek assistance. There are often community organizations, expatriate groups, or even specialized services that can help navigate the bureaucracy and provide guidance.

6. Follow Instructions Carefully: Pay close attention to any instructions provided by officials or on official forms. Making mistakes or overlooking details can result in delays or rejections. Double-check your paperwork before submitting it to ensure accuracy.

7. Keep Records: Make copies of all documents you submit and keep a record of any interactions or communications with officials. This can help you track your progress and provide evidence in case of any discrepancies or issues that arise.

8. Utilize Online Services: In recent years, the French government has made efforts to digitize many bureaucratic processes, offering online portals for tasks such as tax filing, residency applications, and healthcare registration. Take advantage of these services to streamline your experience wherever possible.

9. Understand Cultural Norms: Familiarize yourself with French cultural norms and etiquette when interacting with bureaucrats. Being polite, respectful, and patient can go a long way in smooth interactions and potentially expediting processes.

10. Plan Ahead: Bureaucratic processes in France can often take longer than expected, so it's essential to plan ahead whenever possible. Start gathering necessary documents and initiating processes well in advance of any deadlines or desired outcomes.

By following these tips and approaching French bureaucracy with patience and preparation, you can navigate the system more effectively and minimize stress and frustration along the way.

2.4 Healthcare and Insurance Coverage

France boasts one of the most renowned healthcare systems globally, combining universal coverage with high-quality medical services. The country's healthcare system, known as Sécurité Sociale or "Social Security," is funded through taxes and contributions from both employers and employees. Here's an overview of healthcare and insurance coverage in France:

1. Universal Coverage: France provides universal healthcare coverage to all residents, regardless of their employment status or income level. This ensures that everyone has access to necessary medical services.

2. Public and Private Sector: The healthcare system in France operates through both public and private sectors. Public hospitals and clinics provide a significant portion of healthcare services, while private practitioners and facilities also play a crucial role.

3. Health Insurance: The French healthcare system is primarily financed through a combination of public health insurance and complementary private insurance. Public health insurance covers a substantial portion of medical expenses, including consultations, hospitalizations, and medications. Complementary private insurance, often provided through employers or purchased individually, covers additional costs such as co-payments and services not fully covered by the public system.

4. Carte Vitale: Every resident in France is issued a Carte Vitale, a smart card that contains their personal and medical information. This card simplifies administrative procedures and facilitates reimbursement for medical expenses through the public health insurance system.

5. Reimbursement System: In France, patients typically pay for medical services upfront and then seek reimbursement from their health insurance provider. The reimbursement rates vary depending on the type of treatment and the coverage level provided by the insurance plan.

6. Primary Care: Primary care in France is typically provided by general practitioners (GPs) known as médecins généralistes. Patients have the freedom to choose their primary care physicians, who serve as gatekeepers for accessing specialized care and medical specialists.

7. Specialized Care: Access to specialized medical care, including consultations with specialists and diagnostic tests, is readily available through the French healthcare system. Referrals from primary care physicians are often required for specialized treatments, except in emergencies.

8. Hospital Services: Public hospitals in France offer a wide range of medical services, including emergency care, surgery, and specialized treatments. Patients can choose their preferred hospitals for non-emergency treatments, although proximity and availability may influence their decisions.

9. Prescription Medications: Prescription medications in France are subject to a tiered reimbursement system, with different levels of coverage depending on the drug's classification. Patients may pay a portion of the medication cost at the pharmacy, with the remainder reimbursed by their health insurance.

10. Preventive Care and Public Health Initiatives: France emphasizes preventive care and public health initiatives to promote overall well-being and reduce healthcare costs. Programs targeting vaccination, health screenings, and lifestyle interventions are actively promoted and supported by the government.

In conclusion, France's healthcare and insurance coverage system exemplifies a balance between universal access to medical services and the involvement of private insurers to complement public funding. This comprehensive approach ensures that residents receive high-quality healthcare while minimizing financial barriers to access.

2.5 Taxation and Financial Obligations

Taxation and financial obligations in France are a significant aspect of the country's economic framework, playing a crucial role in funding public services, social welfare programs, and infrastructure development. France has a complex tax system that encompasses various taxes at both the national and local levels, impacting individuals, businesses, and investors. Understanding these tax obligations is essential for compliance and effective financial planning.

1. Income Tax (Impôt sur le revenu):

- France imposes progressive income tax rates on individuals, with higher earners subject to higher rates.
- Income tax is deducted at source for employees through their payslips, while self-employed individuals and those with additional income sources must file annual tax returns.
- Deductions and credits are available for certain expenses, such as childcare, education, and charitable contributions.

2. Value Added Tax (VAT - Taxe sur la valeur ajoutée):

- VAT is a consumption tax levied on most goods and services at each stage of production and distribution.
- France has different VAT rates for various goods and services, with a standard rate of 20% and reduced rates of 10% and 5.5% for essential items like food, transport, and cultural events.

3. Corporate Tax (Impôt sur les sociétés):

- Corporations in France are subject to corporate income tax on their worldwide income.
- The standard corporate tax rate is 28%, but reduced rates apply to smaller companies.
- France offers various tax incentives and credits to encourage research and development, innovation, and investments in certain industries.

4. Wealth Tax (Impôt de solidarité sur la fortune - ISF):

- France used to have a wealth tax, but it was replaced by the real estate wealth tax (Impôt sur la fortune immobilière - IFI) in 2018. IFI applies only to real estate assets exceeding a certain threshold.

- Wealthy individuals may still be subject to a solidarity tax on high incomes (Impôt de solidarité sur les hauts revenus - ISHR) if their income exceeds a certain level.

5. Local Taxes:

- Local authorities levy property taxes (taxe foncière) and residence taxes (taxe d'habitation) on property owners and residents, respectively.
- These taxes fund local services such as schools, waste management, and infrastructure maintenance.

6. Social Security Contributions:

- Both employees and employers contribute to France's social security system, which funds healthcare, pensions, unemployment benefits, and other social welfare programs.
- Social security contributions are calculated as a percentage of salaries and are subject to caps and thresholds.

7. Capital Gains Tax (Impôt sur les plus-values):

- Capital gains tax is imposed on the profit realized from the sale of assets such as real estate, stocks, and bonds.
- The rate of capital gains tax varies depending on the type of asset and the duration of ownership.

8. Inheritance and Gift Tax (Droits de succession et de donation):

- Inheritances and gifts exceeding certain thresholds are subject to taxation in France.
- Tax rates depend on the relationship between the donor and the recipient, with spouses and direct descendants benefiting from exemptions and reduced rates.

9. Compliance and Enforcement:

- The French tax authorities (Direction générale des Finances publiques - DGFiP) are responsible for tax collection, enforcement, and audits.
- Non-compliance with tax obligations can result in penalties, fines, and legal consequences.

In conclusion, navigating the taxation and financial obligations in France requires careful planning and compliance with the country's intricate tax laws and regulations. Seeking professional advice from tax advisors and financial experts can help individuals and businesses optimize their tax strategies while fulfilling their fiscal responsibilities.

Chapter 3

Finding Housing

3.1 Exploring Different Regions and Cities

France is a country renowned for its rich history, diverse culture, picturesque landscapes, and delectable cuisine. From the romantic streets of Paris to the sun-kissed beaches of the French Riviera, each region offers a unique blend of charm and allure. Let's embark on a journey to discover some of the most captivating regions and cities in France.

1. Paris: Known as the **"City of Light,"** Paris is the epitome of romance and sophistication. Iconic landmarks such as the Eiffel Tower, Notre-Dame Cathedral, and the Louvre Museum beckon visitors from around the world. Take a leisurely stroll along the Seine River, indulge in gourmet delights at quaint cafes, or immerse yourself in art at Montmartre's bohemian streets.

2. Provence: Lavender fields, olive groves, and charming hilltop villages define the picturesque region of Provence. Explore the medieval town of Avignon, visit the stunning Palais des Papes, or wander through the vibrant markets of Aix-en-Provence. Don't forget to sample the region's exquisite wines and savory cuisine, infused with fragrant herbs and locally sourced ingredients.

3. French Riviera: Stretching along the Mediterranean coast, the French Riviera exudes glamor and luxury. From the glitzy casinos of Monte Carlo to the pristine beaches of Nice and Cannes, this sun-drenched paradise captivates with its azure waters and vibrant nightlife. Indulge in haute couture shopping along the Promenade des Anglais or unwind in the quaint fishing villages of Antibes and Saint-Tropez.

4. Normandy: History buffs will be enchanted by the charming countryside and historic landmarks of Normandy. Visit the iconic Mont-Saint-Michel, a UNESCO World Heritage Site perched on a rocky island, or explore the D-Day landing beaches, poignant reminders of World War II. Sample local specialties such as Camembert cheese and cider in picturesque villages like Honfleur and Bayeux.

5. Alsace: Nestled along the border with Germany, Alsace boasts a unique blend of French and German influences. Admire the fairytale-like architecture of Strasbourg's old town, home to the magnificent Strasbourg Cathedral and charming half-timbered houses. Explore the picturesque wine route, dotted with quaint villages like Riquewihr and Colmar, renowned for their fine wines and festive Christmas markets.

6. Lyon: Renowned as the culinary capital of France, Lyon delights food lovers with its rich gastronomic heritage. Explore the traboules, hidden passageways weaving through the city's historic center, or wander through the vibrant food markets of Les Halles de Lyon-Paul Bocuse. Don't miss the opportunity to dine at one of Lyon's Michelin-starred restaurants, showcasing the region's culinary excellence.

7. Bordeaux: Wine enthusiasts will be captivated by the vineyard-covered landscapes of Bordeaux, one of the world's most prestigious wine regions. Tour historic chateaux along the Route des Vins, sampling acclaimed wines such as Cabernet Sauvignon and Merlot. Explore the elegant streets of Bordeaux's UNESCO-listed city center, admiring architectural marvels like the Place de la Bourse and Grand Théâtre.

Each region and city in France offers a distinctive blend of history, culture, and natural beauty, inviting visitors to embark on a captivating journey of discovery. Whether you're drawn to the cosmopolitan allure of Paris, the sun-soaked beaches of the French Riviera, or the bucolic charm of the countryside, France never fails to enchant and inspire.

3.2 Renting vs. Buying Property

When it comes to settling in France, whether for a short-term stay or a lifelong commitment, one of the primary decisions expatriates and locals alike face is whether to rent or buy property. Both options offer distinct advantages and drawbacks, influenced by personal circumstances, financial considerations, and long-term goals. Understanding the nuances of renting versus buying property in France is essential for making an informed decision.

Renting Property in France:

1. Flexibility: Renting provides a high degree of flexibility, making it an attractive option for individuals who may not be ready to commit to a specific location or property long-term. Renters can easily relocate to different areas or upgrade to larger accommodations without the financial constraints associated with buying.

2. Lower Initial Costs: Renting typically requires less upfront investment compared to purchasing property. While renters must pay a security deposit and possibly agency fees, these expenses are generally lower than a down payment and closing costs associated with buying a property.

3. Maintenance Responsibility: One of the significant benefits of renting is that tenants are not responsible for major maintenance or repair costs. Landlords typically handle property upkeep, ensuring that tenants can enjoy a hassle-free living experience.

4. Limited Control: Renters have limited control over the property, as any alterations or renovations usually require the landlord's approval. This lack of control may restrict personalization and customization options, making it less appealing for individuals seeking to invest in long-term modifications.

5. Potential Rent Increases: Renters are subject to potential rent increases at the end of each lease term, depending on market conditions and landlord preferences. These fluctuations can make budgeting for housing expenses more challenging and less predictable.

Buying Property in France:

1. Investment Potential: Purchasing property in France can be a sound investment strategy, particularly in popular tourist destinations or areas experiencing gentrification. Property values have historically appreciated over time, providing homeowners with potential long-term financial gains.

2. Stability and Security: Homeownership offers a sense of stability and security, providing individuals and families with a permanent residence and a place to call their own. Owning property can also provide a sense of pride and accomplishment, contributing to overall well-being and satisfaction.

3. Personalization and Control: Unlike renting, homeowners have full control over their property, allowing them to customize and modify their living space to suit their preferences and lifestyle. From renovations to landscaping, homeowners have the freedom to make changes without seeking permission from a landlord.

4. Equity Accumulation: Homeownership allows individuals to build equity over time, as mortgage payments contribute to the gradual ownership of the property. This equity can be tapped into through refinancing or home equity loans, providing homeowners with additional financial flexibility.

5. Responsibility for Maintenance: While homeowners enjoy the benefits of personalization and control, they are also responsible for property maintenance and repair costs. From routine upkeep to unexpected repairs, homeowners must budget for these expenses, which can vary depending on the age and condition of the property.

Deciding whether to rent or buy property in France requires careful consideration of individual preferences, financial circumstances, and long-term goals. While renting offers flexibility and lower initial costs, buying provides stability, investment potential, and greater control over one's living space. Ultimately, the choice between renting and buying depends on factors such as personal preferences, financial resources, and lifestyle priorities. By weighing the advantages and drawbacks of each option, individuals can make an informed decision that aligns with their needs and aspirations in France's dynamic real estate market.

3.3 Understanding Rental Agreements and Contracts

Renting a property in France involves entering into a legally binding rental agreement or lease contract. Whether you're renting a house, apartment, or even a commercial space, it's essential to understand the terms and conditions outlined in the contract to protect your rights and obligations as a tenant. Here's a comprehensive guide to help you navigate rental agreements in France:

1. Types of Rental Contracts:

- **Furnished Rental Contract (Bail Mobilité):** Typically for short-term rentals, usually ranging from one month to one year. This type of contract is suitable for students, temporary workers, or individuals seeking temporary accommodation.
- **Unfurnished Rental Contract (Bail d'habitation):** Usually for long-term rentals, lasting at least one year. It offers more protection to tenants under French law and often leads to a more stable living arrangement.

2. Key Elements of a Rental Agreement:

- **Identification of Parties:** Names and addresses of both the landlord and the tenant.
- **Description of the Property:** Detailed description of the rented property, including its address, size, condition, and any included furnishings or appliances.
- **Duration of the Lease:** Start and end dates of the lease term, including provisions for renewal or termination.
- **Rent Payment Terms:** Amount of rent, frequency of payments, and acceptable methods of payment.
- **Security Deposit:** Amount of the security deposit, conditions for its refund, and any deductions that may be made for damages.
- **Maintenance Responsibilities:** Clarification of which party is responsible for maintenance and repairs of the property and its fixtures.
- **Tenant's Rights and Obligations:** Including rules regarding subletting, noise, and use of the property.

- **Landlord's Rights and Obligations:** Such as providing a habitable dwelling, respecting the tenant's privacy, and giving proper notice before entering the property.

3. Legal Protections for Tenants:

- **Rent Control:** In certain areas, there are regulations in place to limit rent increases.
- **Security of Tenure:** Tenants under an unfurnished rental contract have strong legal protections against eviction without just cause.
- **Notice Periods:** Both landlords and tenants must provide adequate notice before terminating the lease, typically three months for unfurnished rentals.
- **Deposit Protections:** Security deposits must be held in a separate account and returned to the tenant within a specified timeframe, usually within two months after the end of the tenancy.

4. Seeking Legal Advice:

- It's advisable to seek legal advice or assistance from a qualified professional, such as a notary or lawyer, especially when dealing with complex rental agreements or disputes.

5. Understanding Additional Fees:

- In France, tenants may be responsible for additional fees, such as property taxes (taxe d'habitation) or maintenance charges (charges locatives), depending on the terms of the rental agreement.

6. Documentation and Formalities:

- Ensure all agreements and communications with the landlord are in writing to avoid misunderstandings.
- Keep copies of all documents, including the rental agreement, inventory of fixtures, and any correspondence related to the tenancy.

7. Language Considerations:

- If you're not fluent in French, consider having the rental agreement translated into your native language or seeking assistance from a bilingual advisor to ensure you fully understand the terms.

Understanding rental agreements and contracts in France is crucial for both landlords and tenants to ensure a smooth and legally compliant rental experience. By familiarizing yourself with the key elements and legal protections, you can navigate the rental market with confidence and peace of mind.

3.4 Working with Real Estate Agents

Working with real estate agents in France can be a valuable asset whether you're buying, selling, or renting property. France's real estate market can be complex, and having a knowledgeable professional by your side can streamline the process and ensure a successful transaction. Here are some key points to consider when working with real estate agents in France:

1. Licensing and Regulation: In France, real estate agents are regulated by law and must hold a valid license (Carte Professionnelle) issued by the Chamber of Commerce. Make sure to verify that your agent is licensed before engaging in any transactions.

2. Specialization: Real estate agents in France often specialize in specific regions or types of properties. Whether you're interested in a Parisian apartment, a countryside estate, or a coastal villa, look for an agent with expertise in your desired area.

3. Language: While many real estate agents in France speak English, especially in popular tourist areas, it's helpful to work with an agent who is fluent in both English and French. This ensures clear communication and avoids misunderstandings during negotiations.

4. Local Knowledge: A good real estate agent should have in-depth knowledge of the local market, including property values, neighborhood amenities, and legal regulations. They can provide valuable insights and advice to help you make informed decisions.

5. Property Search: Real estate agents can save you time and effort by conducting property searches based on your criteria. Provide them with your preferences regarding location, size, budget, and any specific features you're looking for in a property.

6. Negotiation: Whether you're buying or selling, negotiation skills are crucial in real estate transactions. Your agent can represent your interests, negotiate on your behalf, and help you secure the best possible deal.

7. Legal Assistance: Real estate transactions in France involve complex legal procedures, including contracts, taxes, and title checks. Your agent can guide you through the legal aspects of the transaction and recommend trusted legal professionals if needed.

8. Due Diligence: Before finalizing a transaction, it's important to conduct due diligence to ensure that the property meets your requirements and is free from any legal or structural issues. Your agent can help coordinate inspections and surveys to safeguard your interests.

9. Fees and Commissions: In France, real estate agents typically charge a commission, which is usually paid by the seller. However, it's essential to clarify the terms of engagement and any fees upfront to avoid misunderstandings later on.

10. Professionalism and Trust: Choose a real estate agent who is professional, responsive, and transparent in their dealings. Building a trusting relationship with your agent is key to a successful real estate transaction.

Overall, working with a reputable real estate agent in France can make the buying, selling, or renting process smoother and more efficient. By leveraging their expertise and local knowledge, you can navigate the complexities of the French real estate market with confidence.

3.5 Tips for Finding Affordable Housing

Finding affordable housing in France can be a challenging task, especially in major cities like Paris and Lyon where prices tend to be high. However, with some strategic planning and research, it's possible to find housing options that fit within your budget. Here are some tips to help you find affordable housing in France:

1. Set a Realistic Budget: Before you start your search, determine how much you can afford to spend on rent each month. Take into account other expenses such as utilities, groceries, and transportation.

2. Explore Different Neighborhoods: Prices vary significantly from one neighborhood to another. Consider exploring areas that are less central but still well-connected to amenities and public transportation. These neighborhoods often offer more affordable housing options.

3. Use Online Resources: Take advantage of online platforms and websites dedicated to rental listings in France. Websites like Leboncoin, SeLoger, and PAP (Particulier à Particulier) list a wide range of rental properties, including apartments, houses, and shared accommodations.

4. Consider Shared Accommodations: Sharing a flat or house with roommates can significantly reduce your housing expenses. Look for room rental listings or consider joining housing groups on social media platforms where people advertise available rooms.

5. Look for Social Housing Programs: France has various social housing programs aimed at providing affordable housing to low-income individuals and families. Check with local housing authorities or organizations like Action Logement to see if you qualify for these programs.

6. Negotiate Rent: Don't hesitate to negotiate the rent with landlords, especially if you're renting directly from them rather than through an agency. Landlords may be open to lowering the rent, particularly if the property has been vacant for a while.

7. Consider Alternative Housing Options: In addition to traditional apartments and houses, consider alternative housing options such as studio apartments, studios, and co-living spaces. These options may offer more affordable rent and flexible lease terms.

8. Be Flexible with Your Requirements: Being flexible with your housing requirements, such as the size of the property or specific amenities, can increase your chances of finding an affordable place to live.

9. Stay Informed About Rental Laws: Familiarize yourself with rental laws and regulations in France to ensure you're aware of your rights and obligations as a tenant. Knowing your rights can help you navigate rental agreements and disputes effectively.

10. Seek Assistance from Housing Organizations: If you're struggling to find affordable housing, consider reaching out to housing organizations or non-profit agencies that provide assistance to individuals in need of housing support. They may be able to offer resources, advice, or referrals to affordable housing options.

By following these tips and staying persistent in your search, you can increase your chances of finding affordable housing in France that meets your needs and budget

Chapter 4

Employment and Entrepreneurship

4.1 Researching the Job Market

Researching the job market in France requires a thorough understanding of its economic landscape, industry trends, and cultural nuances. Here's a comprehensive guide to help navigate this process:

1. Economic Overview: Start by familiarizing yourself with France's economic situation. Look into key indicators such as GDP growth rate, unemployment rate, inflation rate, and major industries contributing to the economy. This will give you a broad understanding of the job market's health.

2. Industry Analysis: Identify the industries that are thriving in France. Traditionally, sectors like aerospace, automotive, luxury goods, tourism, technology, and healthcare have been strong. However, trends may shift, so ensure you're up to date with emerging sectors such as renewable energy, biotechnology, and digital services.

3. Job Portals and Websites: Utilize online resources like LinkedIn, Indeed, Glassdoor, and local French job portals such as Monster, Pôle Emploi, and APEC (Association Pour l'Emploi des Cadres) to search for job opportunities. These platforms often provide insights into job openings, company profiles, salary ranges, and hiring trends.

4. Professional Networks: Networking plays a crucial role in the French job market. Join professional groups, attend industry events, and connect with professionals on LinkedIn. Building relationships with people in your field can lead to valuable job opportunities and insights into the job market.

5. Language Skills: Proficiency in French is highly valued in the French job market, even in multinational companies where English is commonly used. Improve your language skills to increase your competitiveness in job applications and daily work interactions.

6. CV and Cover Letter Adaptation: Tailor your CV (curriculum vitae) and cover letter to align with French standards. Emphasize relevant skills, experiences, and achievements. Be concise, professional, and format your documents according to French norms.

7. Understanding Work Culture: French work culture values professionalism, punctuality, and a strong work ethic. Familiarize yourself with cultural nuances such as formalities in communication, hierarchical structures within companies, and the importance of work-life balance.

8. Legal Requirements: If you're not a citizen of an EU/EEA country, familiarize yourself with the legal requirements for working in France. Ensure you have the necessary work permit or visa before applying for jobs.

9. Salary Expectations: Research salary ranges for your desired role and industry in France. Consider factors such as location, experience, and company size when negotiating your salary.

10. Stay Updated: The job market is dynamic, so stay informed about changes in regulations, industry trends, and economic developments that may impact employment opportunities in France.

By following these steps and continuously adapting to the evolving job market dynamics, you can effectively research and navigate job opportunities in France. Remember to leverage your skills, network, and cultural understanding to enhance your prospects of success.

4.2 Seeking Employment Opportunities

France, renowned for its rich cultural heritage, exquisite cuisine, and picturesque landscapes, also offers a myriad of employment opportunities for both its residents and international job seekers. From bustling cities like Paris to charming rural towns, France's diverse economy caters to a wide range of industries, making it an attractive destination for those seeking new professional challenges. This guide aims to provide insights and tips for individuals looking to embark on a career journey in France.

Understanding the French Job Market:
Before delving into job hunting, it's crucial to grasp the dynamics of the French job market. France boasts a strong and diversified economy, with key sectors including aerospace, automotive, technology, tourism, fashion, and healthcare. Additionally, the service industry, particularly hospitality and gastronomy, thrives due to France's status as a global tourist destination.

Language Proficiency:
Proficiency in French is often a prerequisite for many job opportunities in France, especially in customer-facing roles and traditional sectors. While English is widely spoken in multinational companies and certain industries, fluency in French significantly enhances one's employability and integration into the local community. As such, investing time in language courses or immersion programs can greatly benefit job seekers.

Work Permits and Visas:
For non-EU/EEA citizens, obtaining a work permit or visa is necessary to work legally in France. Various types of visas exist, including the long-stay visa for employment purposes (VLS-TS), the EU Blue Card for highly skilled workers, and the Talent Passport for specific professions. It's essential to thoroughly research visa requirements and consult with relevant authorities or immigration lawyers to ensure compliance with regulations.

Networking and Professional Associations:
Networking plays a crucial role in the French job market. Joining professional associations, attending industry events, and leveraging online platforms like LinkedIn can help establish valuable connections and uncover hidden job

opportunities. Additionally, informational interviews with professionals in your field can provide insights into the job market and potentially lead to job referrals.

Job Search Strategies:
Utilize a combination of traditional and digital job search methods when looking for employment in France. While online job boards such as Indeed, LinkedIn, and Monster are popular resources, don't underestimate the effectiveness of networking and spontaneous applications (candidatures spontanées). Tailor your CV (résumé) and cover letter (lettre de motivation) to French standards, highlighting relevant skills and experiences.

Cultural Adaptation:
Adapting to French work culture is essential for successful integration into the workplace. Punctuality, professionalism, and respect for hierarchy are valued traits. Moreover, understanding nuances such as the importance of work-life balance (équilibre vie professionnelle et vie personnelle) and the significance of the lunch break (déjeuner) can positively influence your professional relationships.

Embarking on a career journey in France can be a rewarding experience for those seeking employment opportunities in a vibrant and diverse environment. By understanding the intricacies of the French job market, investing in language proficiency, navigating visa requirements, networking effectively, and adapting to cultural norms, job seekers can maximize their chances of securing fulfilling employment opportunities in France. With determination, patience, and perseverance, your professional aspirations in France can become a reality. Bonne chance! (Good luck!)

4.3 Understanding Work Permits and Contracts

France, with its rich cultural heritage, vibrant economy, and bustling cities, is a popular destination for expatriates seeking employment opportunities. However, before embarking on your professional journey in France, it's crucial to understand the intricacies of work permits and employment contracts to ensure a smooth transition into the workforce.

Understanding Work Permits:

1. Types of Work Permits:

a. Short-Term Work Permit (Autorisation de travail temporaire): Issued for stays less than 90 days.

b. Long-Term Work Permit (Autorisation de travail salarié): Required for stays exceeding 90 days.

c. EU Blue Card: Designed for highly skilled non-EU nationals for long-term residence and work.

d. Seasonal Work Permit: Specifically for temporary work in certain industries like agriculture and tourism.

2. Eligibility Criteria:

a. Long-Term Visa: Obtainable from French consulates or embassies in your home country.

b. Proof of Employment: Typically, you need a job offer from a French employer to apply for a work permit.

c. Qualifications and Skills: Your skills and qualifications must match the requirements of the job.

3. Application Process:

a. Submission of Documents: This includes your passport, proof of employment, educational certificates, and other relevant documents.

b. Processing Time: The duration varies but generally takes several weeks to months.

c. Renewal: Work permits may need to be renewed periodically, depending on the type and duration of employment.

Understanding Employment Contracts:

1. Types of Contracts:

a. CDI (Contrat à Durée Indéterminée): Permanent contract with no fixed end date.

b. CDD (Contrat à Durée Déterminée): Fixed-term contract for a specified duration.

c. CTT (Contrat de Travail Temporaire): Temporary work contract through a staffing agency.

d. Freelance/Independent Contractor: Self-employed individuals who work on specific projects.

2. Key Terms and Conditions:

a. Job Description: Clearly outlines your roles, responsibilities, and reporting structure.

b. Salary and Benefits: Details regarding compensation, bonuses, health insurance, and other perks.

c. Working Hours and Holidays: Specifies working hours, vacation entitlements, and public holidays.

d. Termination Clause: Conditions under which the contract can be terminated by either party.

3. Negotiation and Legal Protection:

a. Legal Rights: French labor laws offer extensive protection to employees, including minimum wage laws and limits on working hours.

b. Collective Bargaining Agreements: Many industries have specific agreements negotiated between employers and trade unions.

c. Seek Legal Advice: It's advisable to consult with a legal expert to ensure your contract complies with French labor regulations and protects your interests.

Navigating work permits and employment contracts in France can be complex, but with proper understanding and preparation, you can embark on a successful professional journey in this captivating country. By familiarizing yourself with the various types of permits, eligibility criteria, and contract terms, you can ensure a smooth transition into the French workforce and enjoy a fulfilling career experience in one of Europe's most dynamic economies.

4.4 Starting a Business in France

Starting a business in France can be an exciting endeavor, offering access to one of Europe's largest and most dynamic markets. However, like any entrepreneurial venture, it requires careful planning, understanding of legal requirements, and knowledge of the business landscape. Here are the key steps to consider when starting a business in France:

1. Market Research and Business Plan:

- Conduct thorough market research to understand the demand for your product or service in France.
- Analyze the competition and identify your unique selling proposition.
- Develop a comprehensive business plan outlining your goals, target market, marketing strategy, and financial projections.

2. Legal Structure:

- Choose the appropriate legal structure for your business, such as a sole proprietorship, partnership, limited liability company (SARL), or corporation (SA).
- Register your business with the appropriate authorities, such as the French Commercial Court (Registre du Commerce et des Sociétés) or the Chamber of Trades (Chambre de Métiers et de l'Artisanat).

3. Business Registration:

- Obtain a SIRET number (French business identification number) from the National Institute of Statistics and Economic Studies (INSEE).
- Register for taxes, including VAT (Value Added Tax) if applicable, with the French tax authorities (Direction Générale des Finances Publiques).

4. Financial Considerations:

- Open a business bank account with a French bank.
- Secure funding for your business through personal savings, loans, grants, or investors.

5. Legal Compliance:

- Comply with labor laws by registering your employees with social security authorities and providing mandatory benefits.

- Ensure compliance with regulations specific to your industry, such as licenses or permits.

6. Intellectual Property Protection:

- Consider trademarking your brand and products to protect them from infringement.
- Safeguard your intellectual property through patents or copyrights if applicable.

7. Language and Cultural Considerations:

- While English is widely spoken in business circles, proficiency in French can be advantageous for networking and navigating bureaucratic processes.
- Familiarize yourself with French business etiquette and cultural norms to build successful relationships with clients, suppliers, and partners.

8. Networking and Support:

- Join business associations, chambers of commerce, and networking groups to connect with other entrepreneurs and access resources.
- Seek guidance from business support organizations such as the French Business Federation (MEDEF) or local Chambers of Commerce and Industry (CCI).

9. Marketing and Promotion:

- Develop a marketing strategy tailored to the French market, including online and offline channels.
- Utilize social media platforms, local advertising, and networking events to promote your business.

10. Adaptability and Persistence:

- Be prepared to adapt your business model based on market feedback and changing regulations.
- Persistence and resilience are essential qualities for navigating the challenges of entrepreneurship in France.

Starting a business in France can be a rewarding endeavor for those willing to invest the time, effort, and resources required. By following these steps and seeking guidance from local experts, you can increase your chances of success in the vibrant French market.

4.5 Networking and Professional Development

Networking and professional development in France are vital aspects of career advancement and personal growth. French professionals place a significant emphasis on building connections, cultivating relationships, and continuously honing their skills to thrive in their careers. Here's an overview of networking and professional development in France:

1. **Networking Culture:** Networking is highly valued in French professional culture. It's common for professionals to attend industry events, seminars, and conferences to expand their professional networks. Additionally, informal networking over coffee or meals is prevalent, providing opportunities for professionals to connect on a more personal level.

2. **Professional Associations:** France boasts numerous professional associations across various industries, offering networking events, workshops, and resources for career development. These associations provide platforms for professionals to exchange knowledge, share experiences, and stay updated on industry trends.

3. **Business Networking Events:** Paris, being a major business hub, hosts numerous networking events regularly. These events range from industry-specific gatherings to general business mixers, allowing professionals to meet individuals from diverse backgrounds and industries.

4. **Online Networking Platforms:** Social media and professional networking platforms like LinkedIn are widely used in France for networking purposes. Professionals leverage these platforms to connect with peers, seek career opportunities, and showcase their expertise.

5. **Professional Development Programs:** French professionals prioritize continuous learning and skill development. Many companies offer professional

development programs, including workshops, training sessions, and certifications, to enhance employees' skills and expertise.

6. Higher Education and Executive Education: France is renowned for its higher education institutions and executive education programs. Professionals often pursue advanced degrees, MBAs, or executive education courses to acquire specialized knowledge and skills relevant to their careers.

7. Mentorship and Coaching: Mentorship and coaching play essential roles in professional development in France. Experienced professionals often mentor younger colleagues, providing guidance, advice, and support to help them navigate their careers more effectively.

8. Language Proficiency: Proficiency in French is often crucial for networking and professional development in France, especially for individuals seeking opportunities in sectors where French is the primary language of business.

9. Cross-Cultural Networking: France's multicultural workforce offers opportunities for cross-cultural networking. Professionals from diverse backgrounds collaborate, exchange ideas, and learn from each other, enriching their professional experiences.

10. Government Support: The French government supports initiatives aimed at fostering professional development and enhancing employability. This support may include subsidies for training programs, incentives for skill development, and policies promoting lifelong learning.

In conclusion, networking and professional development are integral components of the French professional landscape. By actively engaging in networking activities, pursuing continuous learning opportunities, and leveraging available resources, professionals in France can enhance their careers, expand their horizons, and achieve long-term success.

Chapter 5

Education and Family Matters

5.1 Choosing Schools and Universities

Choosing schools and universities in France requires careful consideration of various factors to ensure the best fit for your academic and personal needs. Whether you're a local resident or an international student, here are some key points to keep in mind when making this important decision:

1. **Program Offerings:** Consider the academic programs offered by different schools and universities in France. Determine whether they align with your interests, career goals, and academic aspirations. French institutions are known for their strengths in fields such as engineering, business, fashion, art, and humanities.

2. **Reputation and Rankings:** Research the reputation and rankings of schools and universities in France. While rankings should not be the sole factor in your decision-making process, they can provide valuable insights into the quality of education, faculty expertise, and research opportunities offered by different institutions.

3. **Accreditation:** Ensure that the schools and universities you are considering are accredited by recognized accreditation bodies. Accreditation ensures that the institution meets certain quality standards and that your degree will be recognized both nationally and internationally.

4. **Location:** Consider the location of the institution and its surroundings. France offers a diverse range of environments, from bustling cities like Paris and Lyon to smaller towns and rural areas. Think about factors such as climate, cost of living, cultural attractions, and proximity to potential internship or job opportunities.

5. Language of Instruction: Determine whether the language of instruction at the institution is French or English, depending on your language proficiency and preferences. While many programs are offered in English, particularly at the graduate level, proficiency in French may be beneficial for fully integrating into academic and social life in France.

6. Cost and Financial Aid: Evaluate the cost of tuition, fees, accommodation, and living expenses at different institutions. Additionally, research scholarship and financial aid opportunities are available to international students, including government scholarships, institutional grants, and external funding sources.

7. Student Support Services: Investigate the student support services offered by schools and universities, such as academic advising, career counseling, housing assistance, health services, and extracurricular activities. A supportive campus environment can contribute to your overall academic success and well-being.

8. Internationalization: Consider the level of internationalization and diversity at the institution. Look for schools and universities that have a welcoming and inclusive community, with opportunities for cross-cultural exchange, study abroad programs, and international student support services.

9. Alumni Network and Career Opportunities: Research the alumni network and career services provided by different institutions. A strong alumni network can offer valuable networking opportunities and potential career connections, while comprehensive career services can assist you in finding internships, job placements, and career development resources.

10. Visit and Connect: Whenever possible, visit the campuses of the schools and universities you are considering to get a firsthand look at the facilities, meet faculty and staff, and experience the campus culture. Additionally, reach out to current students, alumni, or admissions representatives to ask questions and gather insights about the institution.

By carefully considering these factors and conducting thorough research, you can make an informed decision when choosing schools and universities in France that align with your academic, personal, and professional goals.

5.2 Understanding the Education System

Understanding the education system in France is essential for both residents and those interested in studying or working in the country. Renowned for its emphasis on academic rigor and excellence, the French education system has a long history and is deeply ingrained in the cultural fabric of the nation. From early childhood education to higher education, the system is structured to provide students with a well-rounded and comprehensive learning experience.

1. Structure of the Education System:

- The French education system is divided into several stages, each with its own unique characteristics and objectives.
- **École Maternelle (Preschool):** This stage is not compulsory but widely attended. It caters to children aged 3 to 6 and focuses on developing social skills, language, and basic cognitive abilities.
- **École Élémentaire (Primary School):** Compulsory for children aged 6 to 11, primary education emphasizes foundational knowledge in subjects like mathematics, French language, science, history, geography, and art.
- **Collège (Middle School):** From ages 11 to 15, students attend collège where they receive a broad education across various subjects. The curriculum becomes more specialized as they progress through the years.
- **Lycée (High School):** High school education lasts for three years (ages 15 to 18) and culminates in the Baccalauréat (commonly known as the Bac), a national exam that determines university eligibility.
- **Higher Education:** Universities, Grandes Écoles, and other specialized institutions offer a range of undergraduate and graduate programs, including vocational and technical courses.

2. The Baccalauréat (Bac):

- The Bac is a crucial milestone in the French education system and serves as both a high school exit exam and university entrance qualification.

- It consists of written and oral examinations in various subjects, with the choice between several streams, including general, technological, and vocational.

- Performance in the Bac determines a student's eligibility for admission to higher education institutions.

3. Specialized Education Institutions:

- France is home to prestigious institutions known as Grandes Écoles, which offer specialized education in fields such as engineering, business, and public administration.

- Admission to Grandes Écoles is highly competitive and often requires completion of preparatory classes known as Classes Préparatoires.

4. Public vs. Private Education:

- The majority of schools in France are public and operated by the government, providing free education up to the university level.

- Private schools, including Catholic schools, also exist and may offer alternative educational philosophies or religious instruction. They often charge tuition fees.

5. Emphasis on Academic Excellence and Rigor:

- The French education system places a strong emphasis on academic achievement, with standardized assessments and rigorous curriculum standards.

- Critical thinking, analytical skills, and mastery of core subjects are prioritized, preparing students for higher education and professional careers.

6. Cultural and Linguistic Education:

- France's education system also emphasizes the preservation of cultural heritage and linguistic proficiency, particularly in the French language.

- Students are exposed to French literature, history, and culture throughout their education, fostering a deep appreciation for the country's heritage.

7. Reforms and Modernization Efforts:

- Like many education systems worldwide, the French system undergoes periodic reforms to adapt to changing societal needs and educational best practices.

- Recent reforms have focused on improving inclusivity, reducing dropout rates, promoting digital literacy, and enhancing vocational training opportunities.

Understanding the intricacies of the education system in France provides valuable insights into the country's cultural values, academic standards, and opportunities for personal and professional growth. Whether pursuing education within France or simply seeking to appreciate its educational heritage, familiarity with the system enriches one's understanding of this vibrant and intellectually rich nation.

5.3 Support Services for Families

In France, support services for families are comprehensive and aim to address various needs ranging from childcare to financial assistance and counseling. These services are designed to alleviate the burdens families may face in balancing work, childcare, and personal responsibilities. Here's an overview of support services available for families in France:

1. Childcare Services: France is renowned for its extensive childcare services, including subsidized nurseries (crèches) for infants and toddlers, preschools (écoles maternelles) for children aged 3 to 6, and after-school programs (centres de loisirs) for older children. These services offer a safe and stimulating environment for children while parents work or attend to other obligations.

2. Family Allowance (Allocations Familiales): The French government provides financial support to families through family allowances. These allowances are provided based on the number of children in the family and the parents' income level. The aim is to help families cover the costs associated with raising children, including education, healthcare, and basic necessities.

3. Parental Leave (Congé Parental): France offers generous parental leave policies to allow parents to spend time with their newborn or newly adopted child. Parental leave can be shared between both parents and is typically up to 16 weeks for the birth or adoption of one child, with additional weeks for multiple births or adoptions.

4. Child Benefits (Prestations Familiales): In addition to family allowances, there are other child benefits available to eligible families, such as the Prime de

Naissance (birth allowance) and the Allocation de Rentrée Scolaire (school supplies allowance). These benefits help parents cover the costs associated with welcoming a new child into the family or preparing for the school year.

5. Family Counseling and Support Services: Various organizations and associations in France provide counseling and support services to families facing challenges such as parenting issues, marital conflicts, or financial difficulties. These services offer guidance, resources, and sometimes therapy to help families navigate through difficult times and strengthen familial bonds.

6. Parenting Classes and Workshops: Community centers, schools, and local government agencies often organize parenting classes and workshops to provide parents with valuable skills and information on child development, effective discipline techniques, and communication strategies. These classes aim to support parents in their role and promote healthy family dynamics.

7. Legal Assistance and Advocacy: Families in need of legal assistance, especially in matters such as custody disputes, domestic violence, or housing issues, can access legal aid services provided by the government or non-profit organizations. These services ensure that families have access to justice and protection of their rights.

8. Specialized Support for Vulnerable Families: For families facing specific challenges such as homelessness, substance abuse, or mental health issues, specialized support services are available through social services agencies, shelters, and rehabilitation centers. These services provide comprehensive assistance tailored to the unique needs of each family.

Overall, France's support services for families reflect a commitment to promoting the well-being and stability of families by addressing their diverse needs and circumstances. These services play a crucial role in fostering a supportive environment for families to thrive and contribute positively to society.

5.4 Childcare Options

In France, childcare options are diverse and cater to the needs of working parents as well as those seeking early childhood education for their children. Here are some common childcare options available in France:

1. Crèches (Daycare Centers):

Crèches are government-regulated child care centers for children aged 2 months to 3 years. They offer full-day care services and typically operate on weekdays. Crèches are known for providing a nurturing environment with trained staff members who facilitate early learning activities and social interaction among children.

2. Micro-Crèches:

Micro-crèches are smaller daycare centers that accommodate fewer children than traditional crèches. They offer similar services but in a more intimate setting, often with a higher caregiver-to-child ratio. This option can be preferable for parents looking for a more personalized approach to childcare.

3. Écoles Maternelles (Preschools):

Écoles maternelles are public preschools for children aged 3 to 6 years. They focus on early education and preparation for primary school. While not solely daycare facilities, écoles maternelles typically offer extended hours to accommodate working parents. These preschools follow the French national curriculum and emphasize play-based learning.

4. Assistants Maternels (Childminders):

Assistants maternels are registered childminders who provide childcare services in their own homes. They offer a more home-like environment for children and often care for small groups of children from various families. This option can be flexible, allowing parents to negotiate hours and services directly with the childminder.

5. Halte-garderies (Drop-in Daycares):

Halte-garderies are drop-in daycare centers where parents can leave their children for short periods, typically a few hours at a time. They are designed to provide temporary care for children while parents attend appointments or run errands. Halte-garderies offer a convenient solution for parents who need occasional childcare support.

6. Parental Co-operatives:

Parental co-operatives, or "crèches parentales," are daycare centers managed by groups of parents who take turns volunteering to care for the children. Parents contribute financially and participate in the operation of the daycare center. This option promotes community involvement and shared responsibility among families.

7. Nannies and Au Pairs:

Some families opt to hire nannies or au pairs to provide childcare in their homes. Nannies are typically professional caregivers who work full-time or part-time, while au pairs are often young adults from foreign countries who live with the family and provide childcare in exchange for room, board, and a stipend.

In France, the government provides financial assistance to families to help cover the cost of childcare, making these options more accessible to a wide range of families. Additionally, childcare facilities in France prioritize safety, quality of care, and early childhood development, ensuring that children receive the support they need during their formative years.

5.5 Adjusting to French Education and Social Norms

Adjusting to French Education and Social Norms can be an enriching yet challenging experience for newcomers to France. Whether you're an international student, an expatriate, or someone relocating for work, understanding and adapting to the nuances of French culture is key to integration. Here's a guide to help you navigate the educational and social landscape:

Education System:

1. Structure: The French education system is highly structured, with a clear progression from primary to secondary to higher education. Understanding this hierarchy can help you choose the right path for yourself or your children.

2. Language: French is the primary language of instruction in most schools and universities. While some institutions offer programs in English, proficiency in French will greatly enhance your academic and social experience.

3. Academic Rigor: French education places a strong emphasis on academic rigor and intellectual debate. Be prepared for challenging coursework and high expectations from teachers and professors.

4. Respect for Authority: Respect for authority figures, including teachers and professors, is deeply ingrained in French culture. Addressing them with appropriate titles (such as "Monsieur" or "Madame") and showing deference in the classroom is expected.

5. Extracurricular Activities: French schools often offer a wide range of extracurricular activities, from sports to arts and culture. Engaging in these activities can help you integrate into the school community and make new friends.

Social Norms:

1. Formality: French society values formality and politeness in social interactions. Using "vous" (formal "you") instead of "tu" (informal "you") with acquaintances and strangers demonstrates respect.

2. Punctuality: Punctuality is highly valued in France. Arriving late to appointments or social gatherings is considered rude, so make an effort to be on time.

3. Personal Space: French people tend to value their personal space and may maintain a greater distance in conversations compared to some other cultures. Respect these boundaries and avoid standing too close.

4. Cuisine: Food is an integral part of French culture, and sharing meals is a common social activity. Embrace the local cuisine and dining etiquette, such as keeping your hands on the table during meals and refraining from starting to eat until everyone is served.

5. Work-Life Balance: French society places a high value on work-life balance, with strong protections for workers' rights. Expect shorter workweeks, generous vacation time, and a focus on enjoying leisure activities outside of work.

Integration Tips:

1. Learn the Language: Invest time in learning French, as proficiency in the language will greatly facilitate your integration into both academic and social settings.

2. Embrace Cultural Differences: Be open to embracing and adapting to cultural differences, whether it's in the classroom, workplace, or social settings.

3. Build Relationships: Seek opportunities to build relationships with locals through shared interests, hobbies, or community activities. Making friends with French natives can provide valuable insights into the culture and help you feel more at home.

4. Stay Patient: Adjusting to a new culture takes time, so be patient with yourself as you navigate the challenges of integration. Celebrate small victories along the way and keep an open mind to new experiences.

By understanding and respecting French education and social norms, newcomers can forge meaningful connections and thrive in their new environment. Embrace the opportunity to immerse yourself in French culture, and you'll find yourself feeling more at home in no time.

Chapter 6

Settling In and Integration

6.1 Establishing a Social Circle

Establishing a social circle in France can be a rewarding experience, offering opportunities for cultural exchange, friendship, and personal growth. Whether you're a newcomer to the country or a long-time resident looking to expand your social network, here are some tips to help you build meaningful connections in France:

1. Language: French is the primary language spoken in France, so proficiency in French can significantly enhance your ability to connect with locals. Consider enrolling in language classes or language exchange programs to improve your fluency and confidence in conversing with others.

2. Community Activities: Get involved in community activities and events to meet people who share similar interests. This could include joining local clubs, sports teams, hobby groups, or volunteering for charitable organizations. French communities often organize festivals, markets, and cultural gatherings, providing ample opportunities to engage with others.

3. Cafés and Bars: French culture places a strong emphasis on socializing in cafés and bars. Spend time frequenting your neighborhood café or bar, where you can strike up conversations with locals over a cup of coffee or a glass of wine. Be open to meeting new people and initiating conversations, as the French generally appreciate friendly interactions.

4. Social Networking: Use social networking platforms to connect with people in your area. Websites like Meetup.com or local Facebook groups often organize gatherings and events tailored to specific interests or communities. Joining online forums or expat groups can also be a useful way to meet fellow expatriates and locals who are open to forming new friendships.

5. Work and Study: If you're working or studying in France, take advantage of opportunities to network with colleagues, classmates, and instructors. Participate in work-related social events, professional networking events, or university clubs to meet people from diverse backgrounds and forge connections within your industry or academic field.

6. Cultural Exchange Programs: Engage in cultural exchange programs that facilitate interaction between locals and newcomers. These programs may involve language exchanges, homestays, or cultural immersion experiences, allowing you to learn about French culture firsthand while forming meaningful connections with locals.

7. Be Open and Respectful: Approach social interactions with an open mind and a genuine interest in learning about the culture and perspectives of others. Respect cultural norms and etiquette, such as observing mealtime customs and practicing good manners. Building trust and rapport takes time, so be patient and persistent in your efforts to establish meaningful connections.

8. Attend Language Classes or Cultural Workshops: Enroll in language classes or cultural workshops offered in your area. These settings provide opportunities to meet fellow learners and enthusiasts who share your interest in French language and culture. Engaging in group activities and discussions can foster camaraderie and lead to lasting friendships.

9. Host Social Gatherings: Take the initiative to host social gatherings or dinner parties, inviting both locals and fellow expatriates. Sharing meals and conversation in a relaxed setting can help break the ice and strengthen bonds between individuals. Consider organizing themed events or potluck dinners to add a fun and interactive element to the gathering.

10. Stay Open-Minded and Flexible: Building a social circle in a new country may come with its challenges, but staying open-minded and flexible in your approach will increase your chances of success. Embrace the opportunity to meet people from diverse backgrounds and be willing to step out of your comfort zone to cultivate meaningful connections in France.

By actively participating in community activities, leveraging social networking platforms, and embracing cultural exchange opportunities, you can gradually establish a fulfilling social circle in France while immersing yourself in the rich tapestry of French culture and society.

6.2 Exploring French Cuisine and Customs

France, renowned for its rich history, cultural heritage, and exquisite cuisine, offers a gastronomic journey like no other. From the bustling streets of Paris to the quaint villages of Provence, every region of France boasts its own culinary traditions and customs, reflecting the diverse landscapes and influences that have shaped the country's food culture over centuries.

French cuisine is celebrated worldwide for its emphasis on fresh, seasonal ingredients, meticulous preparation techniques, and an unwavering commitment to culinary excellence. Here are some highlights of what you can expect when delving into the world of French food and customs:

1. Regional Diversity: France is divided into distinct culinary regions, each with its own specialties and culinary traditions. For example, in Normandy, you'll find creamy camembert cheese and savory apple-based dishes, while Provence offers aromatic herbs, olive oil, and fresh seafood. Exploring these regions allows you to experience the breadth and depth of French gastronomy.

2. The Art of Eating: In France, mealtime is not just about nourishment; it's a ritual to be savored and enjoyed. The French take their time at the table, often lingering over multiple courses accompanied by good conversation and, of course, fine wine. Lunch and dinner are typically leisurely affairs, with an emphasis on quality over quantity.

3. Boulangeries and Patisseries: No exploration of French cuisine would be complete without a visit to a local boulangerie (bakery) or patisserie (pastry shop). Here, you'll find an array of freshly baked bread, flaky croissants, delicate pastries, and decadent desserts that showcase the French passion for baking.

4. Market Culture: French markets are a feast for the senses, offering a vibrant array of seasonal fruits, vegetables, cheeses, meats, and artisanal products. Strolling through a traditional French market provides insight into the importance of fresh, locally sourced ingredients in French cooking.

5. Café Culture: Sidewalk cafés are an integral part of French life, providing a space for people to socialize, relax, and enjoy a cup of coffee or a glass of wine. Whether in a bustling city square or a charming village street, the café culture in France is all about slowing down and savoring the moment.

6. Cheese and Wine Pairings: Cheese and wine are essential components of French gastronomy, and the art of pairing them is taken seriously. With hundreds of varieties of cheese and wines to choose from, the possibilities are endless. Whether it's a creamy brie with a crisp Chablis or a robust Roquefort with a full-bodied Bordeaux, mastering the art of cheese and wine pairing is a delightful adventure.

7. Fine Dining and Haute Cuisine: France is home to numerous Michelin-starred restaurants, where chefs push the boundaries of culinary innovation while still honoring traditional techniques and flavors. Indulging in a gourmet meal at one of these establishments is an unforgettable experience that showcases the pinnacle of French culinary artistry.

In conclusion, exploring French cuisine and customs in France is not just about tasting delicious food; it's about immersing yourself in a cultural experience that celebrates the joys of life, community, and culinary excellence. Whether you're savoring a simple baguette with cheese or dining at a Michelin-starred restaurant, each bite tells a story of tradition, creativity, and passion for good food. So, bon appétit and cheers to the endless delights of French gastronomy!

6.3 Embracing Cultural Events and Traditions

France, a country renowned for its rich cultural heritage, offers a vibrant tapestry of traditions and events that captivate visitors and locals alike. From the grandeur of Bastille Day celebrations to the quaint charm of regional festivals, embracing cultural events and traditions in France is a journey through time and a celebration of diversity.

One of the most iconic events in France is Bastille Day, commemorating the French Revolution. Every July 14th, the streets come alive with parades, fireworks, and festivities, showcasing France's unity and commitment to liberty, equality, and fraternity. The grandeur of military parades along the Champs-Élysées in Paris and the spectacular fireworks illuminating the Eiffel Tower create an electrifying atmosphere that embodies the spirit of the nation.

Beyond national events, France boasts a plethora of regional traditions, each offering a unique glimpse into local culture and history. From the colorful Carnaval de Nice on the French Riviera to the lively Féria de Nîmes in the south, these festivals blend music, dance, gastronomy, and folklore, providing an immersive experience for visitors eager to delve into the heart of French identity.

Cultural events in France extend beyond traditional festivities to encompass art, music, and literature. The Cannes Film Festival, held annually on the French Riviera, attracts filmmakers, actors, and cinephiles from around the globe, showcasing the best of international cinema while celebrating the art of storytelling. Similarly, the Avignon Festival, a world-renowned theater event, transforms the historic city of Avignon into a stage for avant-garde performances and artistic expression.

France's culinary heritage is also deeply ingrained in its cultural fabric, with gastronomic traditions celebrated through festivals and markets across the country.

From the wine harvest festivals in Bordeaux to the truffle markets of Provence, these events offer a sensory journey through France's diverse culinary landscape, inviting visitors to savor the flavors of regional specialties and local delicacies.

In embracing cultural events and traditions in France, one discovers not only the country's rich history but also its ongoing commitment to preserving and celebrating its cultural diversity. Whether witnessing the grandeur of national celebrations or immersing oneself in the rhythms of regional festivals, each experience contributes to a deeper understanding and appreciation of France's cultural heritage.

As visitors and locals alike participate in these events, they become part of a collective narrative that transcends borders and unites people in celebration, reminding us of the power of culture to inspire, connect, and enrich our lives. In France, embracing cultural events and traditions is not merely an act of observation but an invitation to immerse oneself fully in the beauty and vitality of French culture.

6.4 Getting Involved in Local Communities

Getting involved in local communities in France can be a rewarding and enriching experience, offering opportunities to connect with people, contribute positively to society, and immerse oneself in the vibrant French culture. Here are some ways you can get involved:

1. Volunteering: Volunteering is a fantastic way to make a meaningful impact in your local community. Whether it's assisting at a food bank, helping out at a local school, or participating in environmental clean-up projects, there are numerous opportunities to lend a hand. Organizations like Les Restos du Cœur, Secours Populaire, and La Croix-Rouge Française are always looking for volunteers to support their initiatives.

2. Joining Community Groups: Many towns and neighborhoods in France have community groups focused on various interests such as sports, arts, culture, and social causes. Joining these groups not only allows you to pursue your interests but also fosters connections with like-minded individuals. Look for community centers, sports clubs, and cultural associations in your area.

3. Participating in Local Events: French communities often host festivals, markets, and cultural events throughout the year. Attending these events is a great way to engage with your neighbors, learn about local traditions, and support small businesses and artisans. Whether it's a music festival, a culinary fair, or a historical reenactment, there's something for everyone to enjoy.

4. Supporting Local Businesses: Show your support for the local economy by shopping at small businesses, farmers' markets, and independent stores. By buying locally-produced goods and services, you not only contribute to the economic vitality of your community but also help preserve its unique character and heritage.

5. Participating in Civic Activities: Get involved in civic activities such as town hall meetings, neighborhood clean-up campaigns, or community development projects. These activities provide opportunities to voice your opinions, address local issues, and collaborate with fellow residents to create positive change in your community.

6. Learning the Language and Culture: If you're an expatriate or a non-native French speaker, immersing yourself in the language and culture is key to integrating into the local community. Consider taking language classes, attending cultural events, or joining language exchange groups to improve your French skills and connect with native speakers.

7. Supporting Social Causes: Advocate for social causes that are important to you by joining or supporting local advocacy groups, NGOs, or grassroots movements. Whether it's promoting environmental sustainability, advocating for social justice, or supporting marginalized communities, your involvement can make a difference in creating a more inclusive and equitable society.

Overall, getting involved in local communities in France offers numerous opportunities for personal growth, cultural enrichment, and social engagement. By actively participating and contributing to your community, you can foster a sense of belonging, forge meaningful connections, and make a positive impact on the lives of those around you.

6.5 Overcoming Homesickness and Culture Shock

Moving to a new country like France can be an exhilarating adventure filled with opportunities for growth and exploration. However, it's common to experience homesickness and culture shock as you adjust to your new environment. This guide aims to provide practical strategies for overcoming these challenges and embracing your new life in France.

Understanding Homesickness:

Homesickness is a natural emotional response to being away from familiar surroundings, friends, and family. It can manifest as feelings of sadness, loneliness, and longing for home. Recognizing homesickness as a normal part of the adjustment process is the first step in overcoming it.

Tips for Overcoming Homesickness:

1. Stay Connected: Maintain regular communication with loved ones back home through video calls, emails, or letters. Knowing that you have a support system available can provide comfort during difficult times.

2. Build a Support Network: Invest time in forming relationships with locals and fellow expatriates in France. Joining social groups, language exchanges, or community events can help you feel more connected and less isolated.

3. Establish Routines: Create a sense of familiarity and structure in your daily life by establishing routines. Whether it's a morning walk, a favorite café to visit, or a weekly activity, having predictable elements in your schedule can provide stability.

4. Explore Your Surroundings: Immerse yourself in the culture and beauty of France by exploring your new surroundings. Take leisurely walks through picturesque neighborhoods, visit local markets, and indulge in French cuisine to experience the joys of living in this vibrant country.

Understanding Culture Shock:
Culture shock is the disorientation and discomfort experienced when adapting to a new cultural environment. It may include difficulties in understanding social norms, communication barriers, and navigating unfamiliar customs.

Tips for Overcoming Culture Shock:
1. Learn the Language: Investing time in learning French can significantly ease the transition and help you feel more integrated into French society. Enroll in language classes, practice with locals, and immerse yourself in French media to improve your language skills.

2. Educate Yourself: Take the time to learn about French culture, history, and customs. Understanding the cultural nuances and societal norms can help you navigate interactions more smoothly and avoid misunderstandings.

3. Embrace Differences: Approach cultural differences with an open mind and curiosity rather than judgment. Recognize that diversity enriches our experiences and be willing to adapt your perspective to embrace new ways of thinking and living.

4. Seek Support: Don't hesitate to seek support from professionals or support groups if you're struggling with culture shock. Counseling services, expatriate communities, and cultural integration programs can provide valuable resources and guidance.

Adjusting to life in France may present challenges, but with patience, resilience, and a willingness to embrace the unknown, you can overcome homesickness and culture shock. By staying connected, building a support network, exploring your surroundings, learning the language, and embracing cultural differences, you'll not only survive but thrive in your new home. Remember, each challenge you encounter is an opportunity for personal growth and cultural enrichment. Bonne chance!

Chapter 7

Practical Tips for Daily Life

7.1 Transportation and Getting Around

Transportation in France offers a diverse array of options to explore its rich culture, picturesque landscapes, and vibrant cities. From efficient public transport systems to scenic drives through the countryside, here's a guide on getting around in France:

1. Public Transportation: France boasts an extensive and well-connected public transportation network, particularly in major cities like Paris, Lyon, and Marseille. The Paris Metro, for instance, is one of the most efficient subway systems globally, making it easy to navigate the city's attractions. Trams, buses, and regional trains are also prevalent, offering convenient options for traveling within and between cities.

2. TGV (Train à Grande Vitesse): France's high-speed train network, operated by SNCF, is renowned for its speed and efficiency. The TGV connects major cities like Paris, Lyon, Marseille, Bordeaux, and beyond, allowing travelers to cover long distances in a short amount of time. With comfortable seating and frequent departures, it's a popular choice for both domestic and international travel.

3. Regional Trains: In addition to the TGV, France has an extensive network of regional trains (TER) that connect smaller towns and villages. These trains provide an excellent opportunity to explore the country's rural areas, vineyards, and picturesque landscapes at a more leisurely pace.

4. Bicycles: France is also known for its bicycle-friendly infrastructure, particularly in cities like Paris and Bordeaux, where dedicated bike lanes and rental schemes make cycling an attractive option for both locals and tourists. Exploring cities on two wheels offers a unique perspective and allows visitors to discover hidden gems off the beaten path.

5. Driving: While public transportation is excellent in urban areas, renting a car can be a great option for exploring France's countryside and smaller towns. The country's well-maintained road network makes it easy to navigate, and driving allows for flexibility and the freedom to venture off the typical tourist route. Just be mindful of toll roads and parking regulations, especially in urban centers.

6. Walking: France's cities are often best explored on foot, with many attractions, historic sites, and charming neighborhoods easily accessible by walking. Strolling along the Seine in Paris, wandering through the cobblestone streets of Montmartre, or exploring the medieval alleys of Avignon are just a few examples of the delights awaiting pedestrians in France.

7. Boat Cruises: France's extensive network of rivers and canals offers another unique way to explore the country. From leisurely cruises along the Seine in Paris to navigating the picturesque waterways of Burgundy or Brittany, boat tours provide a tranquil and scenic perspective on France's beauty.

8. Air Travel: For longer distances or reaching more remote regions like Corsica or French overseas territories, air travel is often the most practical option. France has numerous airports, including major hubs like Charles de Gaulle Airport in Paris, offering domestic and international flights to destinations across the globe.

Whether you're exploring the vibrant streets of Paris, the sun-soaked beaches of the French Riviera, or the charming villages of Provence, France's transportation options ensure that getting around is both convenient and enjoyable. With a blend of modern infrastructure and timeless charm, traveling in France is an experience to savor.

7.2 Banking and Financial Management

Banking and financial management in France hold significant importance within the country's economy, as France is one of the leading financial centers globally.

From traditional banking services to modern financial innovations, the sector plays a vital role in facilitating economic activities, fostering investment, and ensuring financial stability. Here's an overview:

1. Banking Sector: France boasts a robust banking sector comprising both domestic and international banks. Major players include BNP Paribas, Société Générale, and Crédit Agricole. These banks offer a wide array of services, including retail banking, corporate banking, investment banking, and asset management. French banks operate domestically and have a significant presence in international markets.

2. Regulation and Supervision: The banking sector in France is regulated by the Autorité de Contrôle Prudentiel et de Résolution (ACPR) and the European Central Bank (ECB), as part of the European banking framework. The ACPR oversees the stability of financial institutions and ensures compliance with regulatory standards, promoting consumer protection and financial stability.

3. Financial Markets: France hosts vibrant financial markets, including the Paris Stock Exchange (Euronext Paris), which is one of the largest exchanges in Europe. These markets facilitate the trading of equities, bonds, derivatives, and other financial instruments, providing avenues for raising capital and managing risk for corporations and investors.

4. Fintech Innovation: France has emerged as a hub for financial technology (fintech) innovation, with numerous startups disrupting traditional banking and financial services. These fintech companies offer innovative solutions in areas such as payments, lending, wealth management, and blockchain technology. Regulatory initiatives such as the "French Tech Visa" program aim to attract talent and foster fintech entrepreneurship.

5. Asset Management: France is a major player in the global asset management industry, with firms like Amundi and AXA Investment Managers managing significant assets across various asset classes. Asset management services cater to institutional investors, pension funds, and individual clients, offering investment products tailored to their risk preferences and financial objectives.

6. Islamic Finance: France has also witnessed the growth of Islamic finance, catering to the needs of its Muslim population and attracting investors from the Middle East and beyond. Islamic banks and financial institutions provide Sharia-compliant products and services, adhering to Islamic principles such as prohibition of interest (riba) and investment in ethical assets.

7. Government Initiatives: The French government implements policies and initiatives to promote the competitiveness of the banking and financial sector. This includes fostering innovation through regulatory sandboxes, supporting sustainable finance initiatives, and enhancing cybersecurity measures to safeguard financial systems against cyber threats.

8. International Collaboration: France actively participates in international financial cooperation and regulatory initiatives, collaborating with organizations such as the International Monetary Fund (IMF), the World Bank, and the Financial Stability Board (FSB) to address global financial challenges and strengthen regulatory frameworks.

In summary, banking and financial management in France encompass a dynamic and diversified ecosystem, characterized by a strong regulatory framework, technological innovation, and a global outlook. As the sector continues to evolve, it will play a crucial role in supporting economic growth, fostering innovation, and ensuring financial stability in France and beyond.

7.3 Healthcare System and Accessing Medical Services

France boasts one of the most admired healthcare systems globally, characterized by universal coverage, high-quality care, and accessibility. The country's healthcare system, known as the French National Health Insurance (Sécurité Sociale), ensures that all residents, including foreigners residing or working in France, have access to comprehensive medical services.

Universal Coverage:

The cornerstone of the French healthcare system is its universal coverage, which provides healthcare services to all residents, regardless of their financial status or employment situation. This system is funded through a combination of mandatory social security contributions, taxes, and government subsidies.

Public and Private Healthcare Providers:

France has a mix of public and private healthcare providers. Public hospitals (hôpitaux publics) are funded and managed by the government and offer a wide range of medical services, including emergency care, specialized treatments, and surgeries. Private hospitals (cliniques privées) also play a significant role in the healthcare landscape, providing elective procedures and specialized care.

Primary Care Physicians:

Access to primary care physicians (médecins généralistes) is a fundamental aspect of the French healthcare system. Patients usually register with a general practitioner who serves as their primary point of contact for medical needs. These physicians play a crucial role in preventive care, diagnosis, and referrals to specialists if necessary.

Specialist Care:

Patients requiring specialized medical services can access a wide range of specialists, including dermatologists, cardiologists, neurologists, and more. Referrals from primary care physicians are typically required to see specialists, although patients with private health insurance may have more flexibility in choosing specialists.

Healthcare Access for Expatriates and Visitors:

Expatriates living and working in France are usually covered by the French healthcare system, provided they meet certain criteria and contribute to social security. Additionally, European Union (EU) citizens can access healthcare services in France through the European Health Insurance Card (EHIC) or the new European Health Insurance Card (EHIC).

Emergency Care:

Emergency medical services (SAMU - Service d'Aide Médicale Urgente) are available 24/7 throughout France. In case of a medical emergency, individuals can dial 15 to reach SAMU, where trained professionals provide immediate assistance and, if necessary, dispatch ambulances or other medical resources.

Healthcare Costs and Reimbursement:
While the French healthcare system offers extensive coverage, patients may still encounter out-of-pocket expenses, such as copayments and deductibles. However, most of these costs are reimbursed through the national health insurance system, with supplemental private insurance (mutuelle) available to cover additional expenses and provide enhanced benefits.

Pharmacies:
Pharmacies (pharmacies) are ubiquitous in France, offering prescription medications, over-the-counter drugs, and medical supplies. Pharmacists play a vital role in the healthcare system, providing medication advice, administering vaccinations, and assisting patients with minor ailments.

France's healthcare system stands as a testament to its commitment to ensuring that all residents have access to high-quality medical services. With its universal coverage, comprehensive range of healthcare providers, and emphasis on preventive care, France continues to set a standard for accessible and effective healthcare delivery. Whether for routine check-ups, specialized treatments, or emergency care, residents and visitors alike can trust in the reliability and excellence of the French healthcare system.

7.4 Shopping and Consumer Rights

France, like many other developed nations, has a comprehensive set of laws and regulations in place to protect consumers' rights when shopping. These laws aim to ensure fair and transparent transactions between consumers and businesses, covering various aspects of the shopping experience. Here's an overview of shopping and consumer rights in France:

1. Consumer Protection Laws:

- France has a robust legal framework to protect consumers, including the Consumer Code (Code de la Consommation) and other relevant statutes.
- These laws cover aspects such as product safety, advertising standards, pricing transparency, and consumer contracts.

2. Right to Information:
- Consumers have the right to clear and accurate information about products and services before making a purchase.
- Retailers are required to provide information regarding the price, composition, characteristics, and terms of sale of products.

3. Right of Withdrawal:
- Under French law, consumers generally have a cooling-off period during which they can cancel a purchase made online or through other distance selling methods without providing a reason.
- The cooling-off period is typically 14 days, during which consumers can return the product for a refund.

4. Product Guarantees:
- Consumers are entitled to guarantees on products purchased, ensuring that they are free from defects and suitable for their intended use.
- Guarantees may vary depending on the type of product and its manufacturer, but they generally cover defects and malfunctions.

5. Protection Against Unfair Practices:
- Consumers are protected against unfair commercial practices, such as misleading advertising, aggressive sales tactics, and hidden fees.
- Businesses are prohibited from engaging in practices that could deceive or exploit consumers.

6. Consumer Rights in Disputes:
- In case of disputes between consumers and businesses, consumers have access to various dispute resolution mechanisms.
- This includes mediation services, consumer protection associations, and legal recourse through the courts.

7. Consumer Organizations:

- France has several consumer protection organizations that advocate for consumer rights and provide support and information to consumers.
- These organizations play a vital role in raising awareness about consumer issues and lobbying for policy changes to enhance consumer protection.

8. Online Shopping Regulations:

- Specific regulations govern online shopping in France, including requirements for clear pricing, secure payment methods, and data protection.
- E-commerce businesses operating in France must comply with these regulations to ensure a safe and reliable online shopping experience for consumers.

9. Language Rights:

- Consumers have the right to receive information and contracts in French, as mandated by French law.
- This ensures that consumers can fully understand the terms and conditions of their purchases without language barriers.

10. Enforcement and Penalties:

- Authorities in France enforce consumer protection laws through inspections, investigations, and penalties for non-compliance.
- Businesses found to violate consumer rights may face fines, legal action, and reputational damage.

In conclusion, France has comprehensive legal protections in place to safeguard consumers' rights when shopping. These rights cover various aspects of the shopping experience, including information disclosure, product guarantees, dispute resolution, and online shopping regulations. By upholding these rights, France aims to promote fair and ethical business practices and ensure a high level of consumer trust and confidence in the marketplace.

7.5 Utilities and Home Maintenance

Utilities and home maintenance in France are integral aspects of daily life, ensuring comfort, safety, and efficiency within households. From electricity and water to heating and waste management, French residents rely on various services to maintain their homes. Here's an overview of utilities and home maintenance in France:

1. Electricity (Électricité):

- Electricity is provided by EDF (Électricité de France), the state-owned utility company.
- Most homes in France are powered by electricity, although some rural areas might rely on alternative sources such as propane or solar power.
- Consumption is typically measured in kilowatt-hours (kWh), and bills are issued periodically based on usage.

2. Water (Eau):

- Water supply and sanitation services are managed by local municipalities or private companies.
- Water meters are installed in most homes to measure consumption, and billing is based on usage.
- France has stringent regulations regarding water quality, ensuring that tap water is safe to drink.

3. Heating (Chauffage):

- Heating systems vary depending on the region and individual preferences. Common methods include central heating, electric heaters, and wood-burning stoves.
- Gas heating is also prevalent, with many homes utilizing gas boilers for central heating and hot water.
- Energy efficiency is becoming increasingly important, with incentives for upgrading to more eco-friendly heating systems.

4. Waste Management (Gestion des Déchets):

- France places a strong emphasis on waste management and recycling.
- Most municipalities provide separate bins for different types of waste, including recyclables, organic waste, and non-recyclables.

- Collection schedules vary by location, with regular pickups for each type of waste.
- Recycling is encouraged through education campaigns and incentives.

5. Home Maintenance (Entretien de la Maison):
- Homeowners are responsible for maintaining their properties, including repairs and upkeep.
- Many French households hire professionals for tasks such as plumbing, electrical work, and renovations.
- Regular maintenance is essential to prevent costly repairs and ensure the longevity of the home.

6. Insurance (Assurance Habitation):
- Homeowners and renters are encouraged to have home insurance (assurance habitation) to protect against risks such as fire, water damage, and theft.
- Insurance policies typically cover the structure of the building, as well as personal belongings.
- The cost of insurance varies depending on factors such as location, the value of the property, and the level of coverage.

Overall, utilities and home maintenance play vital roles in maintaining the quality of life in France. With a focus on sustainability and efficiency, the country continues to invest in infrastructure and policies to ensure reliable and environmentally-friendly services for its residents.

Chapter 8

Safety and Legal Rights

8.1 Understanding French Laws and Regulations

Understanding French laws and regulations is crucial for anyone residing or conducting business in France. With its rich legal heritage and complex administrative framework, France has a distinct legal system that governs various aspects of life, including employment, taxation, commerce, and civil rights. Here's an overview to help navigate the intricacies of French law:

1. Civil Law System: France operates under a civil law system, also known as a code-based or Romano-Germanic legal system. The cornerstone of French law is the Napoleonic Code, officially known as the Civil Code (Code Civil), which was established in 1804 and remains the foundation of private law in the country. This code covers areas such as contracts, property, family law, and inheritance.

2. Legal Codes and Legislation: French law is primarily codified, meaning that laws are organized into comprehensive legal codes. Apart from the Civil Code, other important codes include the Commercial Code (Code de Commerce), Labor Code (Code du Travail), and Tax Code (Code Général des Impôts). These codes are regularly updated through legislative processes.

3. Administrative Law: France also has a robust system of administrative law, which governs the relationship between individuals and the state. Administrative law covers areas such as public administration, regulatory agencies, and administrative courts. Key principles include the rule of law, separation of powers, and administrative justice.

4. European Union Law: As a member of the European Union (EU), France is subject to EU laws and regulations. EU law supersedes national law in areas where it has competence, such as competition policy, trade, and consumer protection.

French courts are obligated to uphold EU law and refer cases to the European Court of Justice when necessary.

5. Legal Institutions: The French legal system comprises various institutions responsible for the administration of justice. These include the Constitutional Council (Conseil Constitutionnel), which ensures the constitutionality of laws, the Court of Cassation (Cour de Cassation), the highest court in the judiciary, and administrative courts, such as the Council of State (Conseil d'État).

6. Legal Procedures: Legal procedures in France can be complex and bureaucratic, requiring adherence to formalities and deadlines. It is advisable to seek legal counsel or representation when navigating legal matters, especially those involving litigation or contracts. Legal documents are often written in French, so proficiency in the language is essential.

7. Labor Laws: France has comprehensive labor laws that protect workers' rights and regulate employment relationships. These laws cover areas such as working hours, minimum wage, employee benefits, and termination procedures. Employers must comply with labor standards and collective bargaining agreements.

8. Taxation: The French tax system is complex, with multiple layers of taxation at the national, regional, and local levels. Understanding tax obligations, including income tax, corporate tax, value-added tax (VAT), and social security contributions, is essential for individuals and businesses operating in France.

9. Business Regulations: Entrepreneurs and companies must adhere to various regulations when conducting business in France, including company registration, licensing requirements, intellectual property protection, and competition law. Compliance with commercial regulations ensures legal and ethical business practices.

10. Legal Assistance and Resources: Legal assistance is readily available in France through lawyers (avocats), legal advisors, and public legal aid services. Additionally, official government websites, legal databases, and publications provide valuable resources for understanding and accessing French laws and regulations.

In conclusion, understanding French laws and regulations is essential for individuals, businesses, and institutions operating within the country. By familiarizing themselves with the legal framework, stakeholders can navigate legal challenges, protect their rights, and ensure compliance with applicable laws.

8.2 Knowing Your Legal Rights as an Expat

As an expatriate living in France, it's crucial to be aware of your legal rights to ensure that you can navigate the country's legal system effectively and protect yourself from any potential issues. France, like many countries, has specific laws and regulations that govern various aspects of expatriate life, including residency, employment, healthcare, and more. Here's a guide to help you understand your legal rights as an expat in France:

1. Residency Rights:

- As an expatriate living in France, you must comply with the country's residency requirements. Depending on your nationality and the purpose of your stay, you may need to obtain a visa or residence permit.
- Make sure to familiarize yourself with the different types of residence permits available, such as long-stay visas, temporary residence permits, and permanent residence permits. Each has its own eligibility criteria and application process.
- Keep your residency documents up to date and renew them as required to avoid any legal complications.

2. Employment Rights:

- Expatriates working in France are entitled to certain rights and protections under French labor laws. These include minimum wage requirements, maximum working hours, paid leave, and workplace safety standards.
- Ensure that your employment contract clearly outlines your rights, responsibilities, and compensation package. If you encounter any issues with your employer, seek advice from a legal expert or labor union.

3. Healthcare Rights:

- France has a universal healthcare system that provides coverage to residents, including expatriates who meet certain criteria. You may be eligible for healthcare coverage through the French social security system, depending on your employment status and length of stay.
- Familiarize yourself with the healthcare options available to you, including public health insurance (Assurance Maladie) and private health insurance plans. Understand what services are covered and how to access healthcare in France.

4. Legal Rights and Obligations:

- As an expatriate, you are subject to French laws and regulations, regardless of your nationality. It's essential to understand your rights and obligations under French law to avoid any legal issues.
- Seek legal advice if you're unsure about any aspect of French law or if you encounter legal problems. There are organizations and professionals specialized in assisting expatriates with legal matters.

5. Taxation Rights:

- Expatriates living in France are subject to French taxation on their worldwide income. However, certain tax treaties and exemptions may apply to reduce your tax liability.
- Consult with a tax advisor to understand your tax obligations in France and any available deductions or credits. Make sure to file your taxes accurately and on time to avoid penalties.

6. Cultural Integration and Language Rights:

- Integrating into French society involves respecting its culture, customs, and language. While not legally mandated, learning French can significantly enhance your experience as an expatriate in France and facilitate communication with locals.
- Take advantage of language classes and cultural activities to immerse yourself in the French language and way of life. Being able to speak French can also help you navigate various legal and administrative procedures more easily.

Understanding your legal rights as an expatriate in France is essential for a smooth and successful experience living abroad. By familiarizing yourself with French laws and regulations, seeking appropriate advice when needed, and actively participating in the local community, you can fully enjoy your time in France while safeguarding your rights and interests.

8.3 Safety Tips for Living in France

Living in France can be a delightful experience, but like any country, it's important to prioritize safety to fully enjoy your time there. Here are some safety tips for residents in France:

1. **Be Vigilant in Public Places:** France is known for its bustling cities and tourist attractions. Keep an eye on your belongings in crowded places such as markets, train stations, and tourist sites. Pickpocketing can be a concern, so ensure your bags are securely closed and consider using a money belt for valuables.

2. **Watch Out for Scams:** Unfortunately, scams targeting tourists and residents alike exist in France. Be cautious of strangers approaching you with sob stories or offering unsolicited help, especially in tourist-heavy areas. Common scams include fake petitions, distraction techniques, and "found" jewelry scams.

3. **Stay Informed About Current Events:** Stay updated on any demonstrations, strikes, or protests happening in your area. While demonstrations in France are often peaceful, they can occasionally turn violent or disrupt transportation. Avoid getting caught up in these situations and plan alternative routes if necessary.

4. **Secure Your Home:** Like in any country, home security is essential. Ensure your residence is equipped with sturdy locks on doors and windows. Consider installing a security system or joining a neighborhood watch program if available. Also, be cautious about sharing details of your living arrangements with strangers.

5. **Be Cautious with Transportation:** Whether you're driving or using public transportation, practice caution. Follow traffic laws diligently, and be aware of

aggressive drivers, especially in urban areas. If using public transport, keep an eye on your belongings and be wary of pickpockets, especially during rush hours.

6. Be Aware of Petty Crimes: While violent crime rates in France are relatively low, petty crimes like theft and vandalism can still occur. Avoid leaving valuables unattended in your car or visible in your home, and take precautions when withdrawing money from ATMs.

7. Learn Basic French Phrases: While many people in France speak English, particularly in tourist areas, it's helpful to know some basic French phrases. This not only facilitates communication but also shows respect for the local culture.

8. Emergency Preparedness: Familiarize yourself with the emergency contact numbers in France, including 112 for general emergencies and 17 for police assistance. Keep important documents like passports and medical information in a secure, easily accessible place.

9. Be Mindful of Cultural Sensitivities: Respect cultural norms and customs, particularly when visiting religious sites or participating in local events. Dress modestly when appropriate and be mindful of your behavior in public spaces.

10. Trust Your Instincts: Finally, trust your instincts. If a situation feels uncomfortable or unsafe, remove yourself from it. Whether it's walking alone at night or encountering suspicious individuals, prioritize your safety above all else.

By following these safety tips, you can enjoy your time living in France while minimizing potential risks and ensuring a positive experience in this beautiful country.

8.4 Dealing with Emergencies and Crisis Situations

Dealing with emergencies and crisis situations in France involves a combination of preparedness, response, and recovery efforts at various levels of government and within communities. From natural disasters to security threats, France has established protocols and frameworks to manage a range of crises effectively.

1. Government Response: The French government, through its various agencies and departments, plays a pivotal role in managing emergencies. The Ministry of the Interior oversees civil protection, emergency services, and disaster response. It coordinates with other ministries, such as Defense and Health, to ensure a comprehensive response to crises.

2. Emergency Services: France boasts well-equipped emergency services, including fire brigades (sapeurs-pompiers), medical emergency services (SAMU), and law enforcement agencies (police nationale, gendarmerie). These services are trained to respond swiftly to a variety of emergencies, including natural disasters, terrorist attacks, and public health crises.

3. National Preparedness Plans: France has developed national preparedness plans for various types of emergencies, such as the ORSEC plan for civil protection and the Vigipirate plan for counter-terrorism. These plans outline procedures for mobilizing resources, coordinating response efforts, and disseminating information during crises.

4. Regional and Local Coordination: Crisis management in France is decentralized, with regional and local authorities playing crucial roles. Prefects, appointed by the central government, coordinate emergency response efforts at the regional level, working closely with local mayors, emergency services, and other stakeholders.

5. Communication and Public Awareness: Effective communication is essential during emergencies to disseminate critical information and instructions to the public. France utilizes various channels, including radio, television, social media, and official websites, to keep citizens informed and aware of risks and protective measures.

6. International Cooperation: Given the interconnected nature of crises, France actively participates in international cooperation and assistance mechanisms. This includes collaboration with European Union partners, participation in NATO's defense and security initiatives, and engagement with international organizations like the United Nations and the World Health Organization.

7. Community Resilience: Building community resilience is a priority in France's approach to crisis management. This involves empowering individuals and communities to prepare for and respond to emergencies through education, training, and the promotion of self-help initiatives.

8. Continuous Improvement: France regularly reviews and updates its emergency preparedness and response mechanisms based on lessons learned from past crises and emerging threats. This includes conducting drills, exercises, and simulations to test readiness and identify areas for improvement.

In summary, dealing with emergencies and crisis situations in France involves a multi-faceted approach that encompasses governmental coordination, robust emergency services, public communication, international cooperation, and community resilience-building efforts. By integrating these elements, France aims to mitigate risks, enhance preparedness, and effectively respond to crises as they arise.

8.5 Resources for Legal Assistance and Support

In France, several resources are available to provide legal assistance and support to individuals in need. Whether you're facing a legal issue, seeking advice, or looking for representation, here are some key avenues to explore:

1. Legal Aid (Aide Juridictionnelle): This is a system in France that provides financial assistance to those who cannot afford legal representation. Eligibility is based on income and assets. If you qualify, the government covers all or part of your legal fees. To apply for legal aid, you can contact your local courthouse or legal aid office.

2. Bar Associations (Ordre des Avocats): Each region in France has its own Bar Association, which is a professional organization for lawyers. Bar Associations often provide referral services to connect individuals with qualified attorneys who specialize in the area of law relevant to their case.

3. Legal Clinics (Permanences juridiques): Many cities and towns in France have legal clinics or advice centers where individuals can receive free or low-cost legal guidance from volunteer lawyers. These clinics typically focus on specific legal issues such as housing, employment, immigration, or family law.

4. Legal Assistance Associations (Associations d'aide juridique): There are various non-profit organizations and associations across France dedicated to providing legal assistance and support to disadvantaged or vulnerable groups, such as immigrants, refugees, domestic violence survivors, or people with disabilities.

5. Consumer Rights Organizations (Associations de consommateurs): For issues related to consumer rights, there are organizations like UFC-Que Choisir or CLCV (Consommation Logement Cadre de Vie) that offer legal advice and assistance to consumers facing disputes with companies or service providers.

6. Online Legal Resources: Several websites and platforms offer legal information, self-help guides, and resources in France. These include government websites like Service-Public.fr, which provides information on French laws and procedures, as well as legal forums and communities where individuals can seek advice from legal experts and other users.

7. Notaries (Notaires): Notaries in France play a crucial role in legal matters, especially related to real estate transactions, inheritance, and family law. While notaries primarily handle transactions, they can also provide legal advice and assistance in certain areas.

8. Embassies and Consulates: For foreigners living in France or facing legal issues while visiting the country, embassies and consulates of their respective countries can offer assistance, guidance, and referrals to legal resources or attorneys who speak their language.

9. Mediation Services (Médiation): In some cases, mediation can be an effective alternative to litigation for resolving disputes. There are mediation services available in France that help parties reach mutually acceptable solutions with the assistance of a neutral mediator.

10. Legal Insurance (Assurance de protection juridique): Some insurance policies in France include legal protection coverage, which can help cover legal costs in certain situations. If you have legal insurance, you can contact your insurer to inquire about the services and coverage available to you.

These resources can vary in availability and effectiveness depending on your location, the nature of your legal issue, and your personal circumstances. It's advisable to research and explore multiple options to find the best support for your specific situation. Additionally, consulting with a qualified legal professional is often the most reliable way to address complex legal matters effectively.

Chapter 9

Maintaining Connections with Home

9.1 Staying in Touch with Family and Friends Abroad

In today's interconnected world, distance no longer needs to be a barrier to maintaining meaningful relationships. Living abroad, especially in a culturally rich and diverse country like France, can offer incredible opportunities, but it also presents challenges in staying connected with family and friends back home. However, with the myriad of communication tools and platforms available, nurturing these relationships from afar has never been easier. Here are some strategies for staying in touch with loved ones while living in France:

1. Utilize Messaging Apps: Platforms like WhatsApp, Telegram, or Signal offer instant messaging, voice calls, and even video calls for free. These apps are convenient and can bridge the time zone gap, allowing for real-time communication without incurring international calling charges.

2. Schedule Regular Video Calls: Seeing loved ones' faces can make a world of difference. Set up regular video calls with family and friends back home. Whether it's a weekly catch-up or a special occasion celebration, video calls provide a sense of closeness despite the physical distance.

3. Social Media: Stay connected through social media platforms like Facebook, Instagram, or Twitter. Share updates, photos, and videos of your life in France, and keep up to date with what's happening in the lives of your loved ones abroad. These platforms help maintain a sense of connection and involvement in each other's lives.

4. Send Personalized Messages and Emails: Take the time to send personalized messages and emails to your family and friends. Share your experiences, thoughts, and feelings about living in France, and ask about their lives as well. A heartfelt message can go a long way in maintaining strong relationships.

5. Traditional Communication: Don't underestimate the power of traditional methods of communication, such as letters and postcards. Sending a handwritten note or a thoughtful gift through traditional mail adds a personal touch and shows that you've taken the time to express your love and care.

6. Plan Visits: Whenever possible, plan visits to see your family and friends in person or invite them to visit you in France. Nothing beats spending quality time together and creating lasting memories. Plus, having a future visit to look forward to can strengthen your bond and give you something to anticipate.

7. Join Online Communities: Explore online communities or forums where expats and international residents in France gather. Connecting with others who are going through similar experiences can provide valuable support, advice, and friendship.

8. Celebrate Special Occasions Virtually: Even if you can't be there in person, you can still celebrate special occasions with your loved ones abroad. Host virtual parties, send virtual gifts, or organize online activities to commemorate birthdays, holidays, and other milestones together.

9. Stay Flexible and Understanding: Understand that maintaining relationships across borders requires flexibility and understanding. Time zone differences, busy schedules, and life obligations can sometimes make communication challenging. Be patient and accommodating, and make the effort to stay connected despite the obstacles.

Living abroad in France offers a unique opportunity to immerse yourself in a new culture and lifestyle. While staying connected with family and friends back home may require some effort, the rewards of nurturing these relationships are immeasurable. By leveraging the multitude of communication tools and strategies available, you can bridge the distance and keep your bonds strong across borders.

9.2 Managing Long-Distance Relationships

In the modern world, long-distance relationships have become increasingly common due to various factors such as work, education, or family commitments. For those navigating such relationships in France, a country known for its romance and cultural nuances, managing the distance can present unique challenges. However, with effective communication, trust-building, and thoughtful planning, maintaining a strong connection across miles is entirely achievable.

Clear Communication is Key

Communication lies at the heart of any successful relationship, but it's even more crucial in long-distance scenarios. In France, where emotional expression is often valued, it's essential to openly discuss feelings, concerns, and expectations with your partner. Utilize various communication channels such as video calls, messaging apps, and handwritten letters to stay connected on a personal level despite the physical distance.

Establish Trust and Security

Trust forms the foundation of every healthy relationship, especially when geographical separation is involved. Building trust requires transparency, consistency, and reassurance. In France, where loyalty is highly valued, demonstrating commitment and reliability is essential. Keep each other updated on daily activities, share experiences openly, and make concrete plans for future reunions to foster a sense of security and stability.

Embrace Technology and Creativity

Fortunately, living in the digital age offers an array of technological tools to bridge the gap between partners separated by distance. From virtual date nights to online gaming sessions, leverage technology to create shared experiences and maintain intimacy. Additionally, explore creative ways to surprise and delight your partner from afar, such as sending personalized gifts, planning surprise visits, or scheduling virtual tours of romantic French landmarks.

Prioritize Quality Time Together

While physical proximity may be limited, prioritizing quality time when you're together becomes even more crucial in long-distance relationships. Make the most of your visits by planning meaningful activities, exploring new places, and simply enjoying each other's company without distractions. In France, renowned for its exquisite cuisine and breathtaking scenery, indulge in romantic dinners, leisurely strolls, and memorable adventures to strengthen your bond.

Cultivate Independence and Personal Growth

Maintaining a healthy balance between togetherness and individuality is essential for the success of any relationship, especially in long-distance situations. Use the distance as an opportunity for personal growth, pursue your interests, and nurture your own social circles. Encourage your partner to do the same, respecting each other's autonomy while cherishing the connection you share.

Stay Optimistic and Flexible

Long-distance relationships require patience, resilience, and a positive outlook. Embrace the journey with optimism, focusing on the strengths of your relationship rather than dwelling on the challenges. Remain flexible and adaptable, understanding that plans may change, and obstacles may arise. By approaching difficulties as a team and maintaining a sense of humor, you can navigate the distance together with grace and resilience.

In conclusion, managing a long-distance relationship in France demands dedication, communication, and creativity. By fostering trust, prioritizing quality time, and embracing both independence and togetherness, you can cultivate a strong and enduring connection across the miles. Remember that distance is merely a temporary obstacle on the path to lasting love, and with patience and perseverance, your relationship can thrive regardless of geographical boundaries.

9.3 Celebrating Holidays and Traditions from Home

Celebrating holidays and traditions from home in France holds a special charm, blending centuries-old customs with modern conveniences. Whether it's the vibrant festivities of Bastille Day, the cherished traditions of Christmas, or the delectable delights of Easter, French culture exudes an aura of celebration and togetherness.

Even when circumstances prevent large gatherings or travel, there are numerous ways to revel in the spirit of French holidays from the comfort of home.

1. Bastille Day (14th July):

Known as "La Fête Nationale" or simply "Le Quatorze Juillet," Bastille Day commemorates the French Revolution and the storming of the Bastille in 1789. Despite the grand parades and fireworks typically seen in cities like Paris, you can celebrate from home by hosting a French-themed dinner party. Serve classic dishes like coq au vin or ratatouille, and don't forget the quintessential French wine and cheese. Decorate with blue, white, and red (the colors of the French flag), and cap off the evening with a virtual viewing of fireworks displays.

2. Christmas (Noël):

Christmas in France is a time of magical traditions, from elaborate nativity scenes to festive markets adorned with twinkling lights. At home, you can recreate this ambiance by decorating your space with holly, mistletoe, and a beautifully adorned Christmas tree. Prepare a traditional Réveillon dinner featuring dishes like foie gras, roasted chestnuts, and bûche de Noël (Yule log cake). Exchange gifts on Christmas Eve, following the French tradition, and enjoy a cozy evening with loved ones, perhaps watching classic French films like "Le Père Noël est une ordure" or "La Belle et la Bête."

3. Easter (Pâques):

Easter in France is a delightful blend of religious observance and festive customs, highlighted by chocolate eggs, bells, and the "Easter Monday" holiday. Embrace the spirit of Pâques by organizing an Easter egg hunt in your garden or home, complete with colorful eggs and chocolate treats. Bake traditional Easter pastries like "pains aux raisins" or "pains au chocolat" for a delicious breakfast. Don't forget to decorate eggs with vibrant colors and patterns, a cherished French tradition. Attend virtual church services or watch Easter concerts online to partake in the religious aspect of the holiday.

By embracing these traditions and celebrations from home, you can immerse yourself in the rich tapestry of French culture while creating cherished memories with loved ones. Whether it's through delectable cuisine, festive decorations, or shared experiences, the spirit of French holidays can be joyfully upheld regardless of the circumstances.

9.4 Overcoming Feelings of Isolation and Loneliness

Overcoming feelings of isolation and loneliness can be a challenging journey, especially in a foreign country like France where cultural and language barriers may amplify these emotions. However, there are various strategies and resources available to help navigate and overcome these challenges.

1. **Language Learning:** Improving your French language skills can significantly enhance your ability to connect with others and integrate into the community. Consider enrolling in language classes, joining language exchange groups, or practicing with native speakers through language exchange apps.

2. **Socialize:** Actively seek out social opportunities to meet new people and build connections. Attend local events, join clubs or hobby groups that align with your interests, or participate in community activities. Websites like Meetup.com can be helpful in finding groups with similar interests.

3. **Reach Out for Support:** Don't hesitate to reach out for support from friends, family, or mental health professionals if you're struggling with feelings of isolation and loneliness. There are also support groups and helplines available specifically for expatriates and individuals experiencing loneliness.

4. **Explore the Culture:** Immerse yourself in the local culture by exploring museums, attending cultural events, or participating in traditional activities. Engaging with the culture can help you feel more connected to your surroundings and provide opportunities to meet like-minded individuals.

5. **Volunteer:** Volunteering is a great way to connect with others while giving back to the community. Look for volunteer opportunities in your area, whether it's helping out at a local charity, participating in environmental initiatives, or assisting at cultural events.

6. Stay Active: Physical activity can have a positive impact on your mood and overall well-being. Consider joining a sports club, taking yoga classes, or simply going for regular walks in the park. Exercise not only helps combat loneliness but also provides opportunities to meet new people.

7. Utilize Technology: Stay connected with friends and family back home through video calls, messaging apps, and social media platforms. Additionally, consider joining online forums or expat communities where you can connect with others who may be experiencing similar challenges.

8. Seek Professional Help if Needed: If feelings of isolation and loneliness persist despite your efforts, consider seeking professional help from a therapist or counselor. They can provide support, guidance, and coping strategies to help you overcome these feelings and improve your overall well-being.

Remember that overcoming feelings of isolation and loneliness takes time and effort, but with patience and perseverance, you can build a fulfilling social network and sense of belonging in France.

9.5 Balancing Dual Identities as an Expat

Balancing dual identities as an expatriate in France can be both enriching and challenging. Moving to a new country often means navigating between the culture and traditions of your homeland and those of your adopted country. This experience is particularly pronounced in France, a nation known for its strong cultural identity and rich history.

At the heart of this balancing act lies the tension between preserving one's roots and embracing the culture of the host country. For many expats, maintaining a connection to their home culture is essential for a sense of belonging and identity. This might involve celebrating holidays, cooking traditional foods, or speaking their native language within their expat community.

However, fully integrating into French society also requires embracing its customs and way of life. This could mean learning the language fluently, understanding social norms and etiquette, and immersing oneself in local customs and traditions. Embracing French culture can lead to deeper connections with the local community and a greater sense of belonging.

Yet, finding the balance between these two identities can be challenging. Expats may feel torn between loyalty to their homeland and the desire to fully embrace their new environment. They may also face judgment or misunderstanding from both sides, as they navigate between different cultural expectations.

One strategy for managing this balancing act is to cultivate a sense of cultural fluidity. Rather than viewing their identities as fixed and separate, expats can embrace the idea of being multicultural individuals who can draw from multiple cultural influences. This might involve blending elements of their home culture with aspects of French culture, creating a unique identity that reflects their diverse experiences.

Building a support network of fellow expats and locals can also be invaluable in navigating this journey. Expat communities provide a sense of camaraderie and understanding, while local friends can offer insights into French culture and help expats feel more integrated into their new home.

Ultimately, balancing dual identities as an expatriate in France is a deeply personal journey. It requires openness, flexibility, and a willingness to embrace both the familiar and the unfamiliar. By navigating this path with curiosity and resilience, expats can create a rich and fulfilling life that embraces the best of both worlds.

Chapter 10

Planning for the Future

10.1 Evaluating Long-Term Goals and Aspirations

Evaluating long-term goals and aspirations in France involves understanding the cultural, economic, and social factors that influence individuals' perspectives and ambitions. France, known for its rich history, diverse culture, and strong emphasis on quality of life, presents a unique landscape for evaluating long-term goals and aspirations.

1. Cultural Values: France is deeply rooted in tradition, art, and intellectual pursuits. French society values creativity, innovation, and cultural heritage. When evaluating long-term goals, individuals often consider how their aspirations align with these cultural values. For instance, pursuing a career in the arts, literature, or fashion may be highly regarded.

2. Work-Life Balance: France is known for its commitment to work-life balance and quality of life. The concept of "joie de vivre" (joy of living) is central to French culture. As a result, long-term goals often prioritize achieving a balance between professional success and personal fulfillment. This could involve aspirations related to flexible work arrangements, leisure time, and spending time with family and friends.

3. Education and Career: Education is highly valued in France, with a strong emphasis on academic achievement and intellectual growth. Long-term goals often include aspirations related to education, such as obtaining advanced degrees or pursuing specialized training. Career aspirations may focus on professional development, advancement in one's field, or entrepreneurship.

4. Socio-Economic Factors: Socio-economic considerations play a significant role in shaping long-term goals and aspirations in France. Economic stability, access to resources, and social mobility influence individuals' aspirations. For instance, aspirations related to homeownership, financial security, and retirement planning are common long-term goals for many French citizens.

5. Environmental Consciousness: France places a high priority on environmental sustainability and ecological responsibility. Long-term goals often include aspirations related to environmental conservation, renewable energy, and sustainable living practices. Individuals may aspire to make positive contributions to environmental protection and combat climate change.

6. Global Perspective: France's position as a global leader in politics, economics, and culture influences individuals' long-term goals and aspirations. Aspiring to engage with global issues, participate in international collaborations, or pursue opportunities abroad are common aspirations among many French citizens.

7. Social Justice and Equality: France has a strong tradition of advocating for social justice and equality. Long-term goals may involve aspirations related to activism, community engagement, and fighting against discrimination and inequality. Individuals may aspire to contribute to building a more inclusive and equitable society.

In evaluating long-term goals and aspirations in France, it's essential to recognize the diverse range of factors that shape individual aspirations and the broader societal context in which they exist. By understanding these dynamics, individuals can pursue meaningful and fulfilling long-term goals that align with their values and aspirations within the French cultural framework.

10.2 Investing in French Citizenship

Investing in French citizenship through various means in France can be a strategic move for those seeking to expand their global opportunities, access to the European Union (EU) market, and enjoy the benefits of French residency. France offers several avenues for investors to obtain citizenship or long-term residency, each with its own requirements and benefits.

1. Investment Visas: France offers various investment visa programs designed to attract foreign investors. These visas typically require a substantial investment in the French economy, such as in real estate, businesses, or government bonds. The minimum investment thresholds and requirements may vary depending on the specific visa program.

2. Business Investment: Investing in or starting a business in France can lead to residency or citizenship. The French government encourages entrepreneurial activity through various incentives and support programs for startups and innovative businesses. Investing in a French enterprise not only contributes to the economy but also creates opportunities for obtaining residency or citizenship.

3. Real Estate Investment: Purchasing real estate in France can also pave the way for residency or citizenship. The country's property market, particularly in cities like Paris and Nice, attracts investors from around the world. Buying property in France can offer both a potential return on investment and a path to residency or citizenship, especially through certain investor visa programs.

4. Economic Contribution: Making a significant economic contribution to France, such as through job creation or investment in strategic sectors, can lead to residency or citizenship. This route often involves engaging with French authorities to demonstrate the positive impact of the investment on the local economy and society.

5. Golden Visa Programs: While France does not have a traditional "golden visa" program like some other countries, certain investment pathways can still lead to residency and eventually citizenship. These may include investing in designated sectors or contributing to specific economic development initiatives.

Benefits of French Citizenship:

- EU Access: French citizens enjoy the benefits of being part of the European Union, including the freedom to live, work, and study in any EU member state.

- **Quality of Life:** France is renowned for its high quality of life, excellent healthcare system, rich cultural heritage, and diverse lifestyle options.

- **Education:** French citizens have access to world-class education, including highly regarded universities and institutions, often at subsidized rates.

- **Global Mobility:** French citizenship provides visa-free or visa-on-arrival access to a large number of countries worldwide, facilitating global travel and business opportunities.

- **Political Rights:** Citizens have the right to vote and participate in the democratic process, shaping the future of France and the EU.

Investing in French citizenship is not only a financial decision but also a strategic one that can provide numerous personal, professional, and lifestyle benefits. However, it's essential to thoroughly research the investment options, legal requirements, and potential outcomes before making any significant financial commitments. Consulting with immigration experts, legal advisors, and financial professionals can help navigate the complexities of the process and ensure a successful investment journey towards French citizenship.

10.3 Retirement Planning and Pension Options

Retirement planning and pension options in France are crucial considerations for individuals looking to secure their financial future during their later years. France has a well-established social security system that provides a basic level of retirement income for its citizens. However, many people supplement this with additional private pension plans to ensure a comfortable lifestyle in retirement.

Social Security System:

The French social security system, known as the "Sécurité Sociale," is based on a pay-as-you-go system where current workers' contributions fund the pensions of current retirees. The system provides a basic level of retirement income to all eligible individuals, primarily funded through payroll taxes and contributions from employers and employees.

To be eligible for the full state pension in France, individuals typically need to have worked and contributed to the social security system for a certain number of quarters. The exact requirements depend on factors such as age, number of years worked, and the individual's earnings history.

Additional Pension Plans:
While the state pension provides a foundation for retirement income, many individuals opt for supplementary pension plans to enhance their financial security in retirement. These additional pension plans come in various forms:

1. Occupational Pension Schemes (Retraite Complémentaire): Many employers offer occupational pension schemes to their employees, which supplement the state pension. These schemes may be defined as benefit (where the pension amount is predetermined based on factors like salary and years of service) or defined contribution (where the pension amount depends on contributions and investment performance).

2. Voluntary Personal Pension Plans (Plan d'Épargne Retraite (PER)): Individuals can also set up personal pension plans to save for retirement. The PER system, introduced in 2019, consolidates several existing retirement savings vehicles into a single, flexible plan. Contributions to PER plans are tax-deductible, and withdrawals are taxed as income upon retirement.

3. Individual Retirement Savings Accounts (Plan d'Épargne Retraite Individuel (PERIN)): PERIN is another form of personal pension plan available in France. It allows individuals to make tax-deductible contributions, similar to PER plans, and offers flexibility in investment choices.

4. Retirement Savings Plans (Plan d'Épargne pour la Retraite Collectif (PERCO)):PERCO plans are collective retirement savings plans offered by some employers. Contributions are made through salary deductions, and employers may provide matching contributions. Withdrawals are typically allowed upon retirement, subject to certain conditions.

Tax Treatment:
The tax treatment of pension income in France varies depending on the type of pension and the individual's overall income. State pensions and certain occupational pensions are subject to income tax, while contributions to private pension plans may be tax-deductible. Individuals should consult a tax advisor to understand the tax implications of their pension options.

Retirement planning in France involves a combination of state-provided benefits and supplementary pension plans. While the state pension provides a basic level of income, individuals often opt for additional pension schemes to enhance their retirement savings. Understanding the various pension options and their tax implications is essential for effectively planning for a comfortable retirement in France. Consulting with financial advisors or pension experts can help individuals make informed decisions tailored to their specific needs and circumstances.

10.4 Exploring Opportunities for Further Education or Career Advancement

France, renowned for its rich cultural heritage, exquisite cuisine, and picturesque landscapes, also boasts a robust educational system and vibrant job market. For individuals seeking to advance their education or pursue career opportunities, France presents a plethora of options and advantages. Whether you aspire to enroll in prestigious universities, immerse yourself in French language and culture, or delve into exciting career prospects, exploring opportunities in France can be a rewarding endeavor.

Further Education in France:

1. Acclaimed Universities and Institutions:
France is home to some of the world's most prestigious universities and institutions, offering a wide array of disciplines and programs. Institutions like Sorbonne University, École Normale Supérieure, and Sciences Po Paris are renowned globally for their academic excellence and research contributions. Whether your interests lie in arts and humanities, sciences, engineering, or business, you'll find top-tier educational opportunities in France.

2. Diverse Study Programs:
From undergraduate degrees to doctoral studies, France provides diverse study programs catering to various academic pursuits and career goals. Additionally, many universities offer programs taught entirely in English, making them accessible to international students. Whether you seek a traditional academic curriculum or specialized training in emerging fields, French institutions offer a comprehensive range of options.

3. Cultural Immersion and Language Learning:
Studying in France offers more than just academic advancement—it provides an unparalleled opportunity for cultural immersion and language acquisition. Living in France allows you to immerse yourself in the French way of life, sharpen your language skills, and gain a deeper understanding of French culture and society. This cultural exposure enhances your personal growth and broadens your perspective, preparing you for a globalized world.

Career Advancement in France:

1. Thriving Job Market:
France boasts a diverse and dynamic economy, with opportunities spanning various industries, including technology, healthcare, finance, fashion, and hospitality. Major cities like Paris, Lyon, and Marseille serve as hubs for innovation and entrepreneurship, offering abundant career prospects for skilled professionals. Whether you aspire to work for multinational corporations, startups, or governmental organizations, France's job market is ripe with possibilities.

2. Supportive Work Environment:
French companies prioritize employee welfare and work-life balance, creating a supportive work environment conducive to professional growth and development. Moreover, France's labor laws ensure workers' rights and protections, fostering a sense of security and stability in the workplace. Whether you're starting your career or seeking to advance in your field, France offers a conducive environment for realizing your career aspirations.

3. Opportunities for Innovation and Creativity:
France has a long-standing tradition of innovation and creativity, evident in its contributions to various industries, including technology, fashion, and gastronomy. The country encourages entrepreneurship and invests in research and development, creating fertile ground for innovation and creativity. Whether you're an aspiring entrepreneur, researcher, or creative professional, France provides ample opportunities to turn your ideas into reality.

In conclusion, exploring opportunities for further education or career advancement in France opens doors to academic excellence, cultural enrichment, and professional success. Whether you choose to pursue higher education in prestigious institutions or embark on a rewarding career path in France's vibrant job market, the experiences and opportunities awaiting you are boundless. France's blend of academic excellence, cultural diversity, and economic vitality makes it an ideal destination for those seeking to enrich their lives and advance their careers on both academic and professional fronts.

10.5 Reflections on the Expat Experience and Personal Growth

Moving abroad is often described as a transformative journey, offering a wealth of experiences that can shape one's perspective on life. Among the myriad of destinations, France stands out as a particularly intriguing choice, with its rich cultural heritage, diverse landscapes, and celebrated cuisine. For many expatriates, myself included, the decision to relocate to France is not merely about changing geographical coordinates but embarking on a profound journey of self-discovery and personal growth. In this reflection, I aim to delve into the unique aspects of the expat experience in France and how it has contributed to my personal development.

Cultural Immersion:
One of the most striking aspects of living in France is the immersion into its rich cultural tapestry. From the enchanting cobblestone streets of Paris to the sun-kissed vineyards of Provence, every corner of the country offers a glimpse into its storied past and vibrant present. As an expatriate, embracing French culture goes beyond mere observation; it involves active participation and a willingness to adapt.

Whether savoring a freshly baked croissant at a local boulangerie or engaging in spirited debates at a café, integrating into French life has been instrumental in broadening my horizons and fostering a deeper appreciation for cultural diversity.

Language Acquisition:
Central to the expat experience in France is the journey of language acquisition. While daunting at times, learning French opens the door to meaningful connections and deeper insights into the local way of life. From stumbling through basic conversations to gradually gaining confidence in navigating everyday interactions, each linguistic milestone marks a triumph over the barriers of communication. Beyond practical utility, mastering French has been a gateway to understanding the nuances of French literature, cinema, and art, enriching my cultural experience in profound ways.

Cultural Adjustment:
Adapting to life in a new country inevitably involves navigating the complexities of cultural adjustment. From deciphering social norms to grappling with bureaucratic hurdles, the expat journey is replete with challenges that test one's resilience and adaptability. In France, the concept of "joie de vivre" permeates every aspect of daily life, reminding expatriates to embrace spontaneity and relish life's simple pleasures. While moments of homesickness and frustration are inevitable, they are counterbalanced by the sense of accomplishment that comes with overcoming obstacles and forging meaningful connections in a foreign land.

Personal Growth:
Perhaps the most profound aspect of the expat experience in France is its transformative impact on personal growth. Living outside one's comfort zone fosters a sense of self-reliance and resourcefulness, empowering individuals to confront challenges with courage and resilience. Whether through solo travels across the French countryside or forging friendships with fellow expatriates, every experience becomes a lesson in self-discovery and personal development. Moreover, exposure to diverse perspectives fosters empathy and understanding, broadening one's worldview and instilling a deeper appreciation for the interconnectedness of humanity.

The expat experience in France is a journey of self-discovery, cultural immersion, and personal growth. From navigating the intricacies of language and culture to embracing the joys and challenges of life abroad, every moment is an opportunity for growth and transformation. As I reflect on my time as an expatriate in France, I am reminded of the profound impact it has had on shaping my identity and worldview. Ultimately, the expat journey is not just about geographical relocation but a transformative odyssey that enriches the soul and expands the mind.

Appendices

- Useful Resources and Contacts

1. Emergency Services: In case of emergencies, dial 112 for all emergency services including police, fire, and medical assistance.

2. Embassies and Consulates: For assistance related to visas, passports, and other consular services, contact your country's embassy or consulate in France. Additionally, the French Ministry of Foreign Affairs provides information on diplomatic missions in France for various countries.

3. Tourist Information Centers: These centers offer guidance, maps, and assistance for travelers exploring France. They can provide information on attractions, transportation, and accommodation. Look for the "Office de Tourisme" signs or visit the official website of France Tourism for details.

4. Transportation Hotlines: For inquiries related to public transportation, such as trains (SNCF), buses (RATP), and metros (Métro de Paris), there are dedicated hotlines and websites available. SNCF has a comprehensive website and customer service line for train schedules and bookings.

5. Language Assistance Services: If you encounter language barriers, organizations like the International Federation of Translators and interpreters (FIT) or local language schools can provide translation and interpretation services.

6. Legal Aid and Advice: The French Ministry of Justice provides information on legal aid services available in France. Additionally, there are various legal aid associations and non-profit organizations that offer support to individuals in need of legal assistance.

7. Healthcare Services: The French healthcare system is renowned for its quality. In case of medical emergencies, call 15 for SAMU (Service d'Aide Médicale Urgente). Expatriates and travelers should ensure they have appropriate health insurance coverage.

8. Cultural Institutions: France boasts a rich cultural heritage. For information on museums, galleries, theaters, and cultural events, refer to websites such as the Ministry of Culture or local tourist boards.

9. Business Support Services: Entrepreneurs and businesses can access support from organizations like the Chamber of Commerce and Industry (CCI) and Business France for guidance on regulations, networking opportunities, and market entry strategies.

10. Community and Social Services: There are numerous community centers, non-governmental organizations (NGOs), and volunteer groups offering support in areas such as housing, education, and social integration. Websites like France Bénévolat can help you find volunteering opportunities.

Remember to check official websites and local directories for the most up-to-date information and contacts. Whether you're a tourist, expatriate, or business professional, these resources can help you navigate and enjoy your time in France more effectively.

- Glossary of Key Terms

France, with its rich cultural heritage and diverse society, has a unique set of terms and phrases that are essential to understand its language and culture. Below is a glossary of key terms that are commonly used in France:

1. Bonjour - Literally meaning "good day," this is the standard greeting used throughout France, equivalent to "hello" in English.

2. Merci - This word means "thank you" and is used to express gratitude in various situations.

3. Oui - The French word for "yes."

4. Non - The French word for "no."

5. S'il vous plaît - Translating to "please," this phrase is used to make requests or add politeness to a statement.

6. Au revoir - Meaning "goodbye," this is a polite way to bid farewell to someone.

7. La bise - A common French greeting where people lightly kiss each other on the cheeks, often done between friends or acquaintances.

8. Baguette - A long, thin loaf of French bread, typically with a crispy crust and soft interior.

9. Croissant - A buttery, crescent-shaped pastry that is a staple of French cuisine, often enjoyed for breakfast or as a snack.

10. Fromage - The French word for cheese, which holds a significant place in French gastronomy.

11. Vin - Translating to "wine," France is renowned for its wine production, with regions like Bordeaux, Burgundy, and Champagne producing some of the world's finest wines.

12. Café - In France, this term typically refers to a small cup of strong, black coffee, which is commonly enjoyed throughout the day.

13. Bistro - A small, casual restaurant or café that serves simple and traditional French dishes.

14. Croque-monsieur / Croque-madame - A classic French sandwich made with ham and cheese, often topped with béchamel sauce. A Croque-madame is the same sandwich but topped with a fried egg.

15. Métro - Short for "métropolitain," the Paris Métro is the subway system serving the city of Paris and its suburbs.

16. Château - A French term for "castle" or "manor house," often associated with grand, historic residences in the countryside.

17. Cuisine - Referring to the style or manner of cooking, French cuisine is highly regarded worldwide for its emphasis on fresh, high-quality ingredients and intricate preparation techniques.

18. Mode de vie - Translating to "way of life," this phrase encapsulates the French approach to living, which often emphasizes leisure, gastronomy, and culture.

19. Laïcité - The French principle of secularism, which separates church and state and promotes religious neutrality in public institutions.

20. Joie de vivre - A French phrase meaning "joy of living," representing the appreciation of life's pleasures and the pursuit of happiness.

Understanding these key terms will not only enhance your language skills but also provide insight into the vibrant culture and lifestyle of France.

- Checklist for Relocation to France

Relocating to France can be an exciting adventure, but it also requires careful planning and organization to ensure a smooth transition. Here's a comprehensive checklist to help you manage the process effectively:

Before You Leave:

1. Visa and Immigration:
- Determine the type of visa you need (tourist, work, student, etc.).
- Check the requirements and application process on the official website of the French consulate or embassy.
- Ensure all necessary documents are in order (passport, visa application forms, proof of funds, etc.).

2. Accommodation:

- Research housing options in your desired city or region.
- Contact real estate agents or explore rental websites for listings.
- Arrange temporary accommodation if needed for your arrival.

3. Financial Planning:

- Open a French bank account or ensure your current bank offers international services.
- Notify your bank and credit card companies of your relocation to avoid any issues with transactions abroad.
- Set up automatic bill payments or arrange for a trusted person to handle your finances while you're away.

4. Healthcare:

- Research the French healthcare system and understand your coverage options.
- Obtain necessary health insurance or ensure your current policy covers international healthcare.
- Transfer medical records or obtain copies to bring with you.

5. Language and Cultural Preparation:

- Familiarize yourself with the French language if you're not already proficient.
- Learn about French culture, customs, and etiquette to ease your transition.

6. Documentation:

- Collect important documents such as birth certificates, marriage certificates, academic transcripts, and professional qualifications.
- Ensure all documents are translated into French if necessary and certified for legal use.

Upon Arrival:

1. Residency Registration:

- Register your residence with the local authorities (Mairie) within the required timeframe.

- Obtain a French residency permit if applicable.

2. Utilities and Services:
- Set up utilities such as electricity, gas, water, and internet in your new home.
- Arrange for mail forwarding or update your address with relevant institutions.

3. Transportation:
- Familiarize yourself with public transportation options in your area.
- Apply for a French driver's license if you plan to drive.
- Register your vehicle if bringing one from another country.

4. Healthcare Enrollment:
- Enroll in the French healthcare system if required.
- Choose a primary care physician and schedule any necessary appointments.

5. Banking and Finances:
- Activate your French bank account and obtain necessary debit/credit cards.
- Transfer funds as needed and set up local banking services.

6. Social Security and Taxes:
- Understand your obligations regarding social security contributions and taxes in France.
- Register with the French tax authorities and obtain a tax identification number if required.

7. Education (if applicable):
- Enroll children in schools or childcare facilities.
- Familiarize yourself with the French education system and any requirements for enrollment.

8. Networking and Community Engagement:
- Join local expat groups or community organizations to meet people and integrate into the community.
- Attend cultural events and activities to immerse yourself in the local culture.

Ongoing Maintenance:

1. Legal Compliance:
- Stay informed about any changes to visa regulations, residency requirements, or other legal matters.
- Renew visas or permits as necessary.

2. Language and Integration:
- Continue learning French to improve your communication skills and integration into society.
- Engage with locals and participate in cultural activities to deepen your understanding of French life.

3. Financial Management:
- Keep track of your finances and ensure compliance with French tax laws.
- Review and update your budget as needed to manage living expenses effectively.

4. Health and Well-being:
- Schedule regular health check-ups and maintain any necessary health insurance coverage.
- Stay active and engage in activities that promote physical and mental well-being.

5. Networking and Social Connections:
- Maintain connections with friends, colleagues, and community members.
- Explore new opportunities for socializing and networking to enrich your experience in France.

Relocating to France requires careful planning and attention to detail, but with the right preparation, it can be a rewarding and fulfilling experience. Use this checklist as a guide to ensure a smooth transition and make the most of your time in this beautiful country. Bon voyage et bonne chance!
Checklist for Relocation to France

Relocating to France can be an exciting adventure, but it also requires careful planning and organization to ensure a smooth transition. Here's a comprehensive checklist to help you manage the process effectively:

Before You Leave:

1. Visa and Immigration:

- Determine the type of visa you need (tourist, work, student, etc.).
- Check the requirements and application process on the official website of the French consulate or embassy.
- Ensure all necessary documents are in order (passport, visa application forms, proof of funds, etc.).

2. Accommodation:

- Research housing options in your desired city or region.
- Contact real estate agents or explore rental websites for listings.
- Arrange temporary accommodation if needed for your arrival.

3. Financial Planning:

- Open a French bank account or ensure your current bank offers international services.
- Notify your bank and credit card companies of your relocation to avoid any issues with transactions abroad.
- Set up automatic bill payments or arrange for a trusted person to handle your finances while you're away.

4. Healthcare:

- Research the French healthcare system and understand your coverage options.
- Obtain necessary health insurance or ensure your current policy covers international healthcare.
- Transfer medical records or obtain copies to bring with you.

5. Language and Cultural Preparation:

- Familiarize yourself with the French language if you're not already proficient.
- Learn about French culture, customs, and etiquette to ease your transition.

6. Documentation:

- Collect important documents such as birth certificates, marriage certificates, academic transcripts, and professional qualifications.
- Ensure all documents are translated into French if necessary and certified for legal use.

Upon Arrival:

1. Residency Registration:

- Register your residence with the local authorities (Mairie) within the required timeframe.
- Obtain a French residency permit if applicable.

2. Utilities and Services:

- Set up utilities such as electricity, gas, water, and internet in your new home.
- Arrange for mail forwarding or update your address with relevant institutions.

3. Transportation:

- Familiarize yourself with public transportation options in your area.
- Apply for a French driver's license if you plan to drive.
- Register your vehicle if bringing one from another country.

4. Healthcare Enrollment:

- Enroll in the French healthcare system if required.
- Choose a primary care physician and schedule any necessary appointments.

5. Banking and Finances:

- Activate your French bank account and obtain necessary debit/credit cards.
- Transfer funds as needed and set up local banking services.

6. Social Security and Taxes:

- Understand your obligations regarding social security contributions and taxes in France.

- Register with the French tax authorities and obtain a tax identification number if required.

7. Education (if applicable):

- Enroll children in schools or childcare facilities.
- Familiarize yourself with the French education system and any requirements for enrollment.

8. Networking and Community Engagement:

- Join local expat groups or community organizations to meet people and integrate into the community.
- Attend cultural events and activities to immerse yourself in the local culture.

Ongoing Maintenance:

1. Legal Compliance:

- Stay informed about any changes to visa regulations, residency requirements, or other legal matters.
- Renew visas or permits as necessary.

2. Language and Integration:

- Continue learning French to improve your communication skills and integration into society.
- Engage with locals and participate in cultural activities to deepen your understanding of French life.

3. Financial Management:

- Keep track of your finances and ensure compliance with French tax laws.
- Review and update your budget as needed to manage living expenses effectively.

4. Health and Well-being:

- Schedule regular health check-ups and maintain any necessary health insurance coverage.

- Stay active and engage in activities that promote physical and mental well-being.

5. Networking and Social Connections:

- Maintain connections with friends, colleagues, and community members.
- Explore new opportunities for socializing and networking to enrich your experience in France.

Relocating to France requires careful planning and attention to detail, but with the right preparation, it can be a rewarding and fulfilling experience. Use this checklist as a guide to ensure a smooth transition and make the most of your time in this beautiful country. Bon voyage et bonne chance!

Acknowledgments

Writing a book is not a solitary endeavor; it is a collaborative effort that requires the support and encouragement of many individuals. As I reflect on the journey of creating this guide to relocating to France, I am filled with gratitude for the invaluable contributions of those who have made this endeavor possible.

First and foremost, I would like to express my deepest appreciation to the people of France, whose rich culture, history, and warmth have inspired this book. Your country's beauty and diversity have provided the backdrop for countless adventures and discoveries, and I am honored to share insights into the process of making France your new home.

I am indebted to the experts and professionals who generously shared their knowledge and expertise throughout the research process. Your insights have been instrumental in providing accurate and comprehensive information to readers seeking guidance on navigating the complexities of relocation.

To my family and friends, thank you for your unwavering support and understanding during the countless hours spent researching, writing, and revising. Your encouragement has been a source of motivation, and I am grateful for your patience and belief in this project.

I extend my gratitude to my editor and the publishing team for their guidance and expertise in bringing this book to fruition. Your dedication to quality and attention to detail have been instrumental in shaping the final product.

Lastly, I am profoundly grateful to the readers who will embark on their own relocation journey with the help of this book. It is my sincere hope that the information and insights shared within these pages will empower you to navigate the challenges and embrace the opportunities that come with moving to France.

Thank you to everyone who has played a part, big or small, in bringing this book to life. Your support has been invaluable, and I am deeply appreciative of each and every one of you.

With heartfelt thanks,

Hubert McDonald

Printed in Great Britain
by Amazon